FORMATION IN FAITH

More praise for *Formation in Faith:*

"Grounded in sound scholarship and growing out of Matthaei's lifelong learning in the church, readers are . . . invited to wrestle with new ways of understanding servant leadership and to claim a new vision for being faithful disciples of Jesus Christ in communities of grace in ways that embrace diversity, make connections, build relationships, and sustain creation. . . . This book will be exceptionally useful to me in my ministry and I recommend it highly."
    —Linda J. Vogel, Professor Emerita of Christian Education,
                    Garrett-Evangelical Theological Seminary

"Language is so important in the ways that it shapes us. I celebrate that Sondra Matthaei has identified that 'the language we use to talk about a ministry of forming faith expresses an image and creates a vision for what it is that we are trying to do and why we are doing it.' Language shapes action. We can use her book and its interactive suggestions to engage groups in examining the language we use as we plan and communicate about our ministries."
    —Carolyn Hardin Engelhardt, Church Program Ministries
        Consultant and Director, Ministry Resource Center, Yale
                                    Divinity School

"Sondra Matthaei offers a congregationally based reflection-action process for the formation of disciples of Jesus Christ. She reminds us that disciples, who are formed through authentic relationships within God-centered, faithful, hospitable community, can reach out to the world in servant ministry with a dangerous, norm-challenging presence. Inspiring read!"
    —Ann B. Sherer, Resident Bishop, Nebraska Area, The United
                                    Methodist Church

Formation in Faith

The Congregational Ministry of Making Disciples

Sondra Higgins Matthaei

Abingdon Press
Nashville

FORMATION IN FAITH
THE CONGREGATIONAL MINISTRY OF MAKING DISCIPLES

Copyright © 2008 by Abingdon Press

This book is printed on acid-free paper.

Library of Congress Cataloging-in-Publication Data

Matthaei, Sondra Higgins.
  Formation in faith : the congregational ministry of making disciples / Sondra Higgins Matthaei.
    p. cm.
  Includes bibliographical references (p.   ) and index.
  ISBN 978-0-687-64973-0 (binding: pbk. : alk. paper)
  1. Discipling (Christianity) I. Title.

BV4520.M388 2008
253—dc22

                                                                                2007025964

08 09 10 11 12 13 14 15 16 17—10 9 8 7 6 5 4 3 2 1
MANUFACTURED IN THE UNITED STATES OF AMERICA

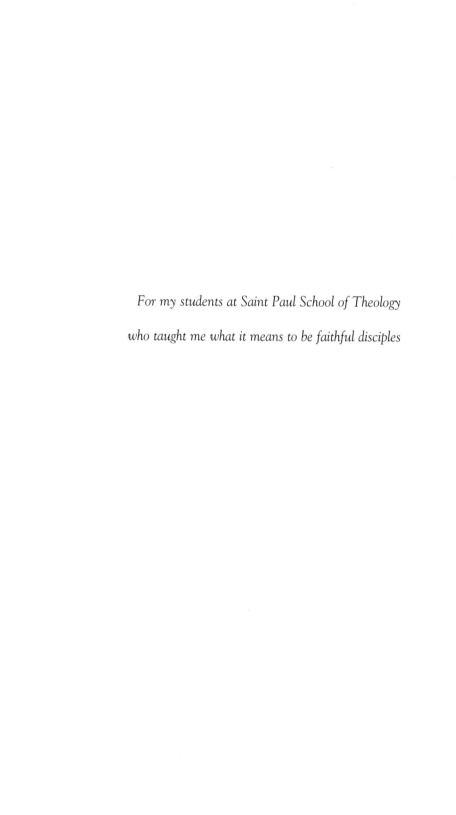

For my students at Saint Paul School of Theology

who taught me what it means to be faithful disciples

Contents

Introduction

I have a passion for the church rooted in seeds that were planted in my childhood. As a member of a parsonage family, I was involved in the church from birth. In reflection, it is clear how my Christian faith and vocation were formed by participating in the full life of the faith community. This experience and passion became an interest, then a local church educational ministry, and now a teaching ministry focused on two basic questions: How do persons become Christian? and How do persons grow in faith?

I believe that persons become Christian through God's love for each one of us made known through the saving work of Jesus Christ and the enabling work of the Holy Spirit. The church's role in this saving and healing work of the triune God is to become a communion of grace focused on carrying on Christ's work in the world. With God's help, a communion of grace lives its life together *as if* the reign of God is already present as it grows in love of God and neighbor. It is in this communion that persons are apprenticed in the Christian life of faith as they learn the rich tradition of the church and practice a Christian way of life in the company of others.

This book is an extension of the research and proposals in my previous book, *Making Disciples: Faith Formation in the Wesleyan Tradition.* In this book, I have attempted to address faith formation for a more diverse expression of Christian traditions, although I admit Wesleyan theology informs my reflection and proposals. In the guided reflections throughout the book, I invite you to use your own theology and denominational perspective in your interpretation of a ministry of forming faith. My thesis remains the same: that congregations need to provide an intentional and unified approach to Christian faith formation so that persons may grow in faithful discipleship and contribute to the renewal of the church's ministry and mission of peace and justice in the world. The focus draws heavily on the Christian tradition, particularly Scripture, while offering concrete proposals for the design and resources for a congregational ministry of forming faith.

In chapter 1, "Relationship, Communion, and Meaning," I address the question of what it is that draws persons into exploring a deeper relationship with God and the church—the longing for authentic relationship, faithful communion, and deeper meaning. This experience of longing is God's invitation into a new relationship as seen in Jesus' encounter with the Samaritan woman. God's invitation calls for a response of loving God and neighbor. A congregational ministry of forming faith cultivates a person's pilgrimage in faith from longing into faithful discipleship.

In chapter 2, "Forming Faith in a Communion of Grace," I propose a vision for a congregational ministry of making disciples and consider the questions, What does it mean to make disciples? How do persons grow in faith? and How does the church grow as a communion of grace? In this chapter, I argue that the life of the faith community itself is the curriculum for forming faith, and I provide insight into what it means to build a communion of grace.

Chapter 3, "Following in the Steps of Love," addresses the question of ministry and leadership in a congregational ministry of forming faith. This chapter challenges the reader to think about ministry as servant ministry, a nonhierarchical partnership of go-betweens on behalf of God and the Christian community. In this ministry every person has gifts to share in the tasks of servant ministry.

The focus of chapter 4, "Growing in Communion with God and All of Creation," is on unity in diversity in the communion of grace as the basis for forming faith. Here I discuss a vision and a plan for a congregational ministry of making disciples—the context and goal, what to teach, who shall teach, and relationships, structures, and practices for forming faith.

In the final chapter, "The Challenges that Lie Ahead," I consider what it means to move forward in love facing the challenges of a congregational ministry of forming faith—creating a vision, building communion, organizing for cultivating the inner and outer lives of faith, assessing the need, and acting in love. I discuss my belief that the servant communion is nourished in the sacrament of Holy Communion and is called to become the bread of Christ for others.

My endeavor in this book has been to continue the vision expressed in *Making Disciples*. The aim of the ministry of Christian faith formation is to make disciples—to nurture Christian identity and Christian vocation so that persons respond to God's grace and find new meaning for their lives in faithful discipleship. A second aim of the ministry of Christian faith formation is to develop the church's role in nurturing and supporting human response to the prompting of the Holy Spirit.[1] It is to this end that I offer this book in the hope that it guides congregations to an ever-deepening love of God and neighbor in a communion of grace where way of life becomes the curriculum for a congregational ministry of making disciples.

Sondra Matthaei
Saint Paul School of Theology
matthaei@spst.edu

CHAPTER ONE

Relationship, Communion, and Meaning

Just then his disciples came. They were astonished that he was speaking with a woman, but no one said, "What do you want?" or, "Why are you speaking with her?" Then the woman left her water jar and went back to the city. She said to the people, "Come and see a man who told me everything I have ever done! He cannot be the Messiah, can he?" They left the city and were on their way to him. (John 4:27-30)

Three women greeted one another as they gathered to meet with me for an afternoon discussion group at Los Angeles City College. We began by reflecting on what the women valued most in their lives. Maria talked about the importance of education and her family. In terms of religion, Maria said, "I am supposedly Catholic. I attended church as a child, but stopped when I got older. I find church boring because I cannot understand what the priest is saying." Maria was further alienated from the church when one of her family members went to confession and the priest scolded the woman rather than talking with her about her concerns. Amelia is focused on finding a better job with more intellectual stimulation. She shared that "enjoying work is what life is all about." Amelia is also seeking a relationship in response to her longing to share life with a partner. In terms of her view of religion, Amelia responded, "I am an atheist, even though I grew up in the church. I received instruction in the faith but found myself questioning what I was taught at an early age. I am emotionally attached to the church, but intellectually, I find it to be nonsense."

Mai finds herself at a big turning point in her life. "I am discovering and appreciating my own identity as a unique human being. I like being in charge of my life, taking risks, and meeting challenges. I focus on the here and now and feel comfortable with the way I am." Mai grew up in the church and sporadically attends church, but now she considers herself to be spiritual, rather than religious. As she said, "I am geared toward developing my spiritual side through integration of body, mind, and spirit."

What is striking about the self-reflection of these three women is that all of them grew up in the church, but none of them finds meaning there now! *Their characterizations of the church include its poor communication of the rich tradition of faith, its lack of openness to questions about life and faith, and its unwillingness to hear the needs of the people.* These are issues that separate the church from people within our congregations, as well as the many people who no longer grace our congregations and those who would never consider entering the doors of the church. These are issues the church must address when creating a congregational ministry of making disciples.

The women's comments highlight the challenges facing congregations as they seek to develop a ministry of Christian faith formation that starts with people where they are in their faith journeys. They call us to a new openness on the part of the church and a new willingness to hear the needs and questions of people around us. This means that members of our congregations need to learn their faith tradition so that they can share it with others. It also means that congregations must cultivate a climate of openness to living in a culture of ambiguity, difference, and change. In other words, *a congregational ministry of Christian faith formation rests on a culture of hospitality.* For noted author and teacher Parker Palmer, hospitality is "receiving each other, our struggles, our *newborn* ideas with openness and care."[1] Welcoming the stranger provides an opportunity for learning and transformation because our lives are enriched by the experiences and ideas of others. This kind of hospitality is part of the biblical tradition of our faith. Palmer writes that in the Bible, "God is always using the stranger to introduce us to strangeness of truth. To be inhospitable to strangers or strange ideas, however unsettling they may be, is to be hostile to the possibility of truth."[2] Put another way, when we turn our backs on a stranger, we are refusing to acknowledge God's presence in our midst and risk losing some of God's truth for our lives. In contrast, life and faith in churches will be enriched when they welcome those who, like Maria, Amelia, and Mai, seek *authentic relationship*, *faithful community*, and *deeper meaning* in their lives.

Authentic Relationship

We often meet or hear of people who say they are searching for authentic relationship. We have some idea of what they mean and have a sense that it is important for the church and Christian faith formation, but what are they seeking? Having all the answers is not what seems to be most important, but offering companionship on the journey is the key. Authentic relationships with persons in the church are critically important in stopping the loss of those who find the church to be irrelevant. As I met with Maria, Amelia, and Mai, I realized that *hearing is the beginning of authentic relationship*. The definition of "to hear" points to the fact that hearing starts with the ear, but it follows with the deeper listening of the heart. The move from hearing to listening coincides with Harvard educator Laurent Daloz's comment that listening is "actively engaging with [another person's] world and attempting to experience it from the inside."[3] Authentic relationship involves this kind of interactive listening that begins with hearing and the opportunity to be heard. So, for the purposes of this book, I am using the word *hearing* to signify this dual meaning—hearing with the ear and listening with the heart. When persons feel that others are really trying to hear and to understand their stories in this way, a relationship becomes meaningful to them.

Being heard, being known, and being accepted are the characteristics of authentic relationships. When others accept us as we really are, we come to know ourselves in new ways. John Zizioulas, a Greek Orthodox scholar, writes: "The significance of the person rests in the fact that [a person] represents two things simultaneously which are at first sight in contradiction: particularity and communion. . . . A person cannot be imagined in [herself or] himself but only within his [or her] relationships."[4] In other words, humans do not thrive in isolation. In the interaction of relationships, persons come to know themselves, and their identity and faith is shaped through those relationships. In fact, Erik Erikson, a developmental theorist, argues that caring relationships are needed throughout life, but are particularly critical for infants from birth in order to nurture *basic trust*.[5] The importance of basic trust is that it becomes the seed of faith that later enables persons to trust God.

Authentic relationships give purpose and meaning to our lives as we discover ourselves in them. As Palmer observes, "We have forgotten that the self is a moving intersection of many other selves. We are formed by the lives which intersect ours. The larger and richer our community, the larger and richer is the content of the self. There is no individuality without community."[6] So in a congregational ministry of making disciples the church's role is to welcome others and to listen to their stories, needs, interests, questions, and ideas in order that they come to know that they are a valued part of God's creation. If, through inattention or criticism, the church repeatedly communicates that a person is unfaithful or unworthy to be a part of the Christian community, it is likely that he or she will take on that image. Maria and Amelia both learned that to question is to be unfaithful because of the way their churches responded. But the reverse is also true. When a person is heard, with encouragement and support, that person can grow in faithfulness. Then the process of forming faith is enhanced.

To listen deeply and to hear the heart of another person is a gift beyond measure. Nelle Morton, a feminist theologian, recorded an experience in 1971 when a woman who had been silent during an entire workshop began to speak on the final day. As the woman told her story, everyone in the group listened. No one interrupted. No one tried to help her find the right words. When the woman finished her story, Morton reports, "Her eyes narrowed then moved around the group again slowly as she said: 'I have a strange feeling you heard me before I started. You heard me to my own story. *You heard me to my own speech.*'"[7] When someone really hears us, we find our voice to speak, to tell our story, and to learn something about who we are and where we belong. In other words, persons discover themselves through the experience of speaking and being heard. This new experience of being heard becomes being known. To be known and then accepted is a gift of grace that opens people to growing in faith as part of a faithful community.

Thinking, Reflecting, Acting

Search "authentic relationship" on the Internet to see what you find.

Think of a song that describes authentic relationship for you and list the characteristics of the relationship from the song.

Interview a friend or relative about how they would define "authentic relationship" and ask where they have found this kind of relationship.

A Faithful Community

Maria, Amelia, and Mai were seeking not only authentic relationships but also faithful communities that heard and accepted them. When we are open to the voices of others, *hearing builds community*, particularly community with those who are different from ourselves. Hearing the stories of others opens up the possibility of finding connection through shared experience or feelings. For example, as I listened to the stories of the Mayan people of Guatemala who had lost family members in the violence there, I could not imagine what it would be like to stand in their shoes, but I could find connection in the feelings of pain and loss. By being silent and listening, I was drawn into their community as one who now knew their story and stood with them in their pain.

In the introduction to *First, We Must Listen: Living in a Multicultural Society,* Anne Leo Ellis writes, "First, we must listen. Carefully, thoughtfully, without interruption, without hidden agendas, without preconceptions. Next we need to think. And talk. With each other. As openly as possible, prepared for misunderstanding and anger, but also for healing, comprehension, reconciliation— friendship."[8] In other words, Ellis is describing an intentional process of listening, thinking, talking, and healing. In order to practice this kind of interactive listening, we must be aware of ourselves first—our biases, prejudices, assumptions, and expectations. It requires an act of trust on our part to be silent in the presence of another person. And it is an act of faith to believe that a child of God is before us, a person who very well might be a vehicle of God's grace in our lives. This was certainly the case in my experience with the Mayan people. The testimony of their faithfulness, in spite of the horrible violence in their lives, witnessed to God's faithfulness in times of trial and transformed my life.

Hearing not only helps persons come to new self-awareness and self-understanding but also *transforms community into communion.* It is common practice to use the word *community* to name our "experience in relationships" when we feel especially close to others.[9] From a sociological point of view, Evelyn and James Whitehead understand community as a "style of group life."[10] This definition uses *community* to name a group of people to which we belong, such as our workplace, school, or neighborhood—a "structure" of community.[11] Parker Palmer sees these groupings of people not as self-selected but as a God-given gift: "In a true community we will not choose our companions, for our choices are so often limited by self-serving motives. Instead, our companions will be given to us by grace. Often they will be persons who will upset our settled view of self and world. In fact, we might define true community as that place where the person you least want to live with always lives!"[12] In other words, our neighbors and the people we see every day are the community given to us by God, and they become the way God meets us in our daily lives.

To use the word *communion* points to something deeper than our individual or sociological understanding of community. When we recognize that God is a participant in these relationships, community becomes communion as persons are heard, known, and accepted through the development of authentic relationships within our churches. A sense of interdependence, shared faith, and a concern for the well-being of each member of the faithful community are qualities of communion. In other words, communion is a deep mutual sharing in the lives of others, or as John Zizioulas describes it, "a fundamental interdependence."[13]

Communion begins with hearing because it is in the hearing and then the listening that we find mutual authentic relationship. All of us have had the experience of speaking to persons who are not really listening to us. They may be attentive and offer affirmative comments, but we know when they start speaking that they have not really heard anything we were saying. As a result, we do not experience any real connection with them. Living in communion requires that we listen with our hearts to those around us. And in communion, there is space for individuality and difference in the midst of our common life in the Christian tradition. We are bound together in communion by our shared life, but there is also room to celebrate the unique gifts of each member of that communion. And communion brings deeper meaning to our lives.

Thinking, Reflecting, Acting

Discuss with a friend what "faithful community" means to you.

Name all the communities to which you belong. Which ones would you describe as "faithful?"

Where have you seen, heard, felt, or experienced communion in community?

What songs or hymns characterize the image of faithful community for you?

Find examples of faithful community in the newspaper, on the Internet, on TV, or in the movies.

Deeper Meaning

Meaning is an essential element in what people call "authentic relationship" because these relationships help us make sense of our world. Religious educator Charles Foster writes that "when something has meaning, we have *a sense of being at home* with the subject."[14] Whether it is a relationship or an experience or an idea, it is meaningful if it resonates with our experience through our reflection on that experience. Our life together in faithful community offers the possibility of finding deeper meaning for our lives.

In everyday life, as well as in times of special challenge, *hearing nurtures meaning.* To hear the story of another person provides an opportunity for meaning-making. Meaning is an interpretation of our life experience that begins with telling our stories and naming our experience. Jack Mezirow, an educational theorist who has written extensively about meaning, observes: "Our need to understand our experiences is perhaps our most distinctively human attribute."[15] In other words, we want to make sense of our lives so we use our values, beliefs, and previous life experience to interpret events and experiences as they happen. We incorporate those interpretations into our life story. In *Yearning for God,* Christian educators Margaret Ann Crain and Jack Seymour share responses from numerous interviews with lay persons. Through this reflection process, persons were heard to speech as they shared their life stories and discussed faith questions. Reflecting on the gratitude expressed by the participants for their listening, Crain and Seymour observe, "We found these people hungering for an opportunity to reflect on the meaning of their lives and relationship with God through deep and thorough conversation."[16] In the telling and in the hearing, authentic relationship was created, faithful community was shared, and new or renewed meaning was discovered. And the telling did not happen in an isolated event but in the midst of faithful community.

> **Thinking, Reflecting, Acting**
>
> Where have you found the deepest meaning for your life? What made this experience significant?
>
> Name one question of meaning you would like to discuss with another person.

God's Invitation

As we have discovered, hearing marks the beginning of authentic relationship with others. Hearing is also the beginning of our relationship with God. For in the beginning, God not only created us, *God heard us*. Nelle Morton describes her realization of the insight that God heard us before God spoke, "Ah! No! In the beginning was not the Word. In the beginning was the hearing."[17] In other words, God heard and knew the deepest needs of creation before God spoke a word of redemption and salvation. God created us in love, cares for us in love, and invites us into a new relationship in love.

We find witness to God's hearing in Scripture. In the story of the Samaritan woman (John 4:1-42), the disciples expressed astonishment that Jesus was talking not just to a woman but to a *Samaritan* woman (v. 27-30). As the story goes, Jesus was traveling through Samaria and stopped to ask the woman at the well for a drink. The woman responded, "How is it that you, a Jew, ask a drink of me, a woman of Samaria?" (v. 9). The fact that Jesus even spoke to the woman was counter to social, cultural, and religious norms in the long-established divide between the Jews and the Samaritans. As New Testament scholar Frances Taylor Gench observes, "Jesus is presented as deliberately crossing this ethnic and religious boundary."[18] And even more shocking is the extended discussion that Jesus has with the woman about her life and God's promise of eternal life. Gench argues in her contextual analysis that this is a symbolic rather than a historical account with the

Samaritan woman representing the Samaritan people because "in the course of her extended conversation with Jesus, she raises a variety of religious and theological issues that were key matters of dispute between Jews and Samaritans (see vv. 9, 12, 20)."[19]

Whether we side with the argument for symbolic or historical interpretation, what we observe in Jesus' conversation with the woman at the well adds to our image of a God who first hears the needs of God's people and then offers redemption. Gench writes that "in the first round of their conversation (vv. 7-15), we learn that [Jesus] crosses boundaries between male and female, and between chosen and rejected people, demonstrating that the grace of God is available to all."[20] The acceptance demonstrated in Jesus' boundary-crossing is the first movement toward establishing trust so that stories can be shared and heard—the beginning of authentic relationship. Gench continues, "In the second round of their conversation (vv. 16-26), Jesus continues to draw the Samaritan woman to faith, with a reference to her marital history that illustrates his ability to see what is inside a person. Stunned by Jesus' extraordinary knowledge of her life, the woman is now able to see him with new eyes."[21] Here, the experience of being heard, being known, and being accepted frees the Samaritan woman to see not only Jesus in a new way but also herself—it is a moment of self-discovery and transformation for her. And this transformation leads to witness and invitation for others to meet Jesus.

The story of Jesus and the Samaritan woman reassures us that while we might experience times when we are estranged from God, God is faithful to us and never abandons us. God hears us and knows us because God has given us everything that we are and have—our gifts, our shortcomings, our longings, our hopes. So we, like the Samaritan woman, along with Maria, Amelia, and Mai, are God's children from birth. God's unconditional love hears us into being. And when we sin, God hears our pain and speaks—grace. This grace is God's invitation to deeper relationship and comes to us as a result of God's hearing our need for authentic relationship, faithful community, and deeper meaning. In other words, God forgives us for our unfaithfulness and invites us into a new relationship through Jesus Christ and the presence of the

Holy Spirit so that we might live in communion with God and all of creation.

Our Response

It is now clear that establishing an authentic relationship in-volves an invitation *and* a response. God's hearing and offering of unconditional love invites us to respond in faith, and Scripture provides us guidance about that response: "'You shall love the Lord your God with all your heart, and with all your soul, and with all your mind.' This is the greatest and first commandment. And a second is like it: 'You shall love your neighbor as yourself'" (Matt 22:37-39). What this commandment tells us is that it is not enough to have a personal and private relationship with God, even if we love God with all our hearts. We love God by loving our neighbor, by loving God's creation as much as God does. While this statement is easy to say, it is much more difficult to live when we ask, Who is our neighbor? For John Wesley, the founder of my denominational tradition, the answer is clear: "If any [person] ask, 'Who is my neighbour?' we reply, 'Every [person] in the world.'"[22] From this point of view, every human being is our neighbor—even those we might be reluctant to love.

The challenge in Wesley's statement is reframed in a contem-porary study of the great commandment by New Testament scholar, Warren Carter, who discusses the "dangerous love" in-herent in the command to love God and neighbor. In his in-depth analysis of this commandment, Carter highlights the political, re-ligious, and social conflict in the early New Testament commu-nity and names the consequences for truly loving God and neighbor:

> Jesus' commands to love God and neighbor are not unique, but they are dangerous. They point to a way of life in which com-mitment to God and to just human interaction are intricately connected. They set out a way of life profoundly committed to God's vision for societal structure that is at odds with and

challenges self-serving power, status, and wealth—then and now. They envision a world in which, contrary to much business as usual, all know the goodness of God's life-giving provision for God's creation.[23]

This picture of a way of life that calls us to put loving God and God's creation first before power, status, and wealth is a commitment to a dangerous love that challenges social and political norms in society.

Jesus' conversation with the Samaritan woman is an example of dangerous love and what it means to hear, know, and accept all persons we meet in our daily life, including the outcast and those some would call "unacceptable." The beginning of authentic relationship and transformation is found in the act of Jesus' hearing the Samaritan woman. In the relationship was an invitation into a community of the faithful, and in the discussion was the source of deeper meaning in the woman's life.

Thinking, Reflecting, Acting

How are you like the Samaritan woman? Why?

What would you want to talk to Jesus about?

Where do you see dangerous love at work in our world today?

A Congregational Ministry of Forming Faith

In this chapter, we have heard the need of our neighbors for authentic relationship, faithful community, and deeper meaning. And we have been reminded of God's love for and faithfulness to all of creation. The question now is, How could we construct a ministry of forming faith that will welcome people like Maria, Amelia, and Mai—or the Samaritan woman? If our goal for Christian faith formation is to cultivate faithful discipleship, then pastors and leaders in the church need to attend carefully to those around us who no longer find relevance or meaning in the church. We are challenged to create a congregational ministry of making disciples so persons might discover *authentic relationship, faithful community*, and *deeper meaning for their lives* in the church. These three critical issues are at stake in our world and in the church's ministry of Christian faith formation.

In order to create a congregational ministry of forming faith, we draw on the resources of the Christian tradition to shape our response to this need, including Scripture, the history of the church, and the symbols and rituals of our faith. We believe that we are created by God to be in relationship with God and all of creation and that God accompanies the search for authentic relationship, faithful community, and deeper meaning. We know that our capacity for relationship is a God-given gift that leads us toward communion.

The church's ministry of forming faith is about helping others hear God's invitation to relationship and then respond to God's grace through faithful discipleship. Jesus' encounter with the woman at the well provides a model and a challenge for a forming faith. Jesus' openness to this theological discussion illustrates one way that this process develops from the first moment of recognizing the woman at the well through the discussion to the point of transformation and witness to others—a process of forming faith. *We could describe the steps in the faith formation process between Jesus and the Samaritan woman as making connection, hearing the story, drawing out questions of faith, entering into honest conversation, and challenging the woman to a new vision.* The result of this interaction is transformation and new life. Out of this account, we could conclude that relationship with Jesus and with each other is at the heart of Christian discipleship, a vocation of loving God and neighbor.

In this book, I am proposing that a congregational ministry of forming faith begins with hospitality, hospitality for each other and hospitality for the stranger. It continues with a willingness to hear each other's stories, to nurture our life together as a faithful community, and to cultivate authentic relationships with God and others that lead to deeper meaning for our lives. While the need for authentic relationship, a faithful community, and deeper meaning for life is essential to planning a congregational ministry of forming faith across the whole life span, this book focuses on the critical period of adulthood and on those persons beyond the membership of our churches who are seeking deeper meaning in life. *Ultimately, I am arguing that our goal is to participate in God's work of transformation and new life so that persons may grow in faithful discipleship through love of God and neighbor.*

Toward Creating a Congregational Ministry of Making Disciples

RELATIONSHIP, COMMUNION, AND MEANING

Discuss the main ideas of this chapter with your planning team for a congregational ministry of making disciples. What insights have you gained? What questions do you have?

The Need in Our World

Authentic relationship: being heard, being known, being accepted

Faithful community: culture of hospitality, climate of openness to God's truth in the stranger, growing in communion

Deeper meaning: an interpretation of life experience that gives us a sense of being at home

God's Invitation

God created us in love, cares for us in love, and invites us into a new or deeper relationship.

Jesus' interaction with the Samaritan woman is an example of God's invitation.

Our Response

The dangerous love of following Jesus puts loving God and God's creation first before power, status, and wealth.

Hear, know, accept all persons we meet in our daily life including the outcast and those some would call "unacceptable."

A Congregational Ministry of Forming Faith

Goal: to cultivate faithful discipleship, a vocation of loving God and neighbor

Resources: Christian tradition—Scripture and history—and life experience

Process or Method: making connection, hearing the story, drawing out questions of faith, entering into honest conversation, challenging a new vision

Hope: transformation and new life

Other Suggestions for Reflecting and Planning

These suggestions can be used for individual reflection, for discussion in a Christian education event for youth or adults, or for sharing with a team who is designing a congregational ministry of making disciples.

Personal Experience in the Church

Share with others:

- How you came to be involved in the church. What were the reasons for your involvement?
- Discuss what you value most about your church.
- How would you describe your relationship with the church?
- Have you every felt alienated from the church? If so, in what way?
- Can you think of a time when you felt heard and accepted in the church?
- Where do you find the primary meaning for your life?

Your Church and Its Community

To discover the needs of your community and how your church can respond to those needs:

- Use the Internet to find out who lives in your church's neighborhood (demographics from census reports and so on).

∾ Create a map of where your church members live.

∾ Interview your neighbors in the church neighborhood to find out (a) what people know about your church, (b) how your church could be helpful to them, and (c) what they have to offer the church.

∾ Does your church welcome others—or not? Ask a friend who has not attended your church to come to church alone and observe what is welcoming and what is not. (You can have lunch together afterwards.) Or you could visit another church alone to see what is welcoming and what is not to get clues about how to be a hospitable congregation.

∾ Do a Bible study of the woman at the well to discern more insights for your congregational ministry of forming faith.

∾ On a board, assess your congregational life by brainstorming answers to the following questions.

	AUTHENTIC RELATIONSHIP	FAITHFUL COMMUNITY	DEEPER MEANING
Where do you find these things in your congregation?			
Where do you see the need for these things in your congregation?			
How could you create these things in your congregation?			

Additional Reading for This Chapter

Hospitality

Nouwen, Henri J. M. *Reaching Out: The Three Movements of the Spiritual Life.* New York: Doubleday, 1975.

Palmer, Parker J. *To Know as We Are Known: A Spirituality of Education.* San Francisco: Harper & Row, 1983.

Communion

Dean, Kenda Creasy, and Ron Foster. *The Godbearing Life: The Art of Soul Tending for Youth Ministry.* Nashville: Upper Room Books, 1998.

Felton, Gayle Carlton. *Mystery: A United Methodist Understanding of Holy Communion.* Nashville: Discipleship Resources, 2004.

Palmer, Parker J. *The Promise of Paradox: A Celebration of Contradictions in the Christian Life.* Notre Dame, Ind.: Ave Maria Press, 1980.

Willimon, William H. *Sunday Dinner.* Nashville: Upper Room Books, 1994.

C H A P T E R   T W O

Forming Faith in a Communion of Grace

---

*For just as the body is one and has many members, and all the members of
the body, though many, are one body, so it is with Christ. For in the one
Spirit we were all baptized into one body—Jews or Greeks, slaves or free—
and we were all made to drink of one Spirit.*

*Indeed, the body does not consist of one member but of many. . . . As it is,
there are many members, yet one body. The eye cannot say to the hand, "I
have no need of you," nor again the head to the feet, "I have no need of
you." On the contrary, the members of the body that seem to be weaker are
indispensable, and those members of the body that we think less honorable
we clothe with greater honor, and our less respectable members are treated
with greater respect; whereas our more respectable members do not need this.
But God has so arranged the body, giving the greater honor to the inferior
member, that there may be no dissension within the body, but the members
may have the same care for one another. If one member suffers, all suffer together with it; if one member is honored, all rejoice together with it.*
(1 Cor 12:12-14; 20-26)

To my teenage eye, Mrs. Anderson was beyond comprehension.
How could anyone be so good? was a frequent thought in my skep-
tical mind. Mrs. Anderson had been the senior-high Sunday school
teacher for years, and it fell to her to be my teacher too. Other than
the fact that she called on me to pray every Sunday because I was the
preacher's kid and that the class was not very stimulating, I could
find no fault. This plain-spoken and patient teacher was a model of
the Christian life. By her words and actions, she communicated to us
that she was a Christian in "heart and life" as John Wesley put it.[1] In
other words, she loved God with her whole heart, and she loved us.

I do not know what struggles and temptations Mrs. Anderson had faced in her lifetime, but I could see that she participated fully in the life of the church, particularly through the women's organization. She was always in worship. She was faithful to her teaching responsibilities, always present and always prepared, and she invited the senior-high class into her home for meals and discussions. For a brief time, she journeyed with us as we explored our faith, and I have never forgotten her. Although I am sure that Mrs. Anderson was not perfect, the way she lived her life and related to a group of active teenagers was most formative in my life.

Vision and Goal

This adolescent experience begins to create a vision of forming faith for me: *a congregational ministry of making disciples is not about creating perfect people, but it is about helping persons grow into faithful disciples who walk through life's challenges and opportunities loving God and neighbor.* In 1742, John Wesley offered one description of what it means to live a Christian life:

> [A person] is a Christian, not in *name* only, but in *heart* and in *life*. [A Christian] is inwardly and outwardly conformed to the will of God, as revealed in the written Word. *[A Christian] thinks, speaks, and lives according to the* 'method' *laid down in the revelation of Jesus Christ.* His [or her] soul is 'renewed after the image of God', 'in righteousness and in all true holiness'. And 'having the mind that was in Christ' he [or she] 'so walks as' Christ 'also walked'.[2]

In this vision of the Christian life, a person is Christian in both *heart*, the inner life of loving God, and *life*, the outer life of loving God by loving one's neighbor. This Christian life is guided by Scripture and follows the way of Jesus in thinking, speaking, and living. And with God's help, a faithful disciple walks as Jesus walked. But how would we describe what it is that signals a faithful life for our time? What do we hope will be the result of our ministry of Christian faith formation? What characteristics or qualities of faith and discipleship would we name? What does it mean to be conformed to the will of God and to be transformed for Christlike living? Before we design a ministry of forming faith, we need to know what it is that we are trying to accomplish.

Scripture shows us the way to a faithful life. So we could name one goal for forming faith as having the heart of a Christian, loving God with all our heart, soul, and mind (Matt 22:37-38). This means accepting the guidance of Scripture as "the *only and sufficient* rule both of Christian faith and practice," one of the "*distinguishing marks*" of the Christian life according to John Wesley.[3] In other words, believing that Scripture contains all that we need to know about God's promises and what God wants us to do with our lives is evidence of our love of God. A second mark of the Christian life for Wesley was that faith is more than "opinion."[4] In other words, faith is based in knowledge and understanding of God's will as revealed in Scripture, meaning that it is important to read widely and discuss what it means to be faithful in terms of following the guidance of Scripture. Because Christians come from different cultural and theological perspectives, this mark affirms that active debate about theological issues in the interpretation of Scripture only serves to deepen one's faith. In other words, there is more than one way to love God with all our heart and mind, so loving God also means that we are willing to wrestle with the meaning of God's Word in Scripture for our own lives. Faith means loving God with our minds.

When we grow in our inner life of faith, we come to love God more deeply with our whole being through our words and actions. To keep God's commandments and to obey God's will is a demonstration of Christian love for God and what God has done in Jesus Christ. Loving God means that we strive to do good and avoid doing harm to ourselves, others, or creation.[5] In other words, we love God by participating in God's intention for creation by avoiding life-destroying practices and joining in life-giving practices using the gifts that God has given us to lead a faithful life. These marks of the Christian life are guides for those who are growing in the inner life of faith.

Christians are known not only by their inner faith of loving God but also by their outer lives of loving their neighbor. The commandment to love God and neighbor serves as the guide and rule for a Christian's heart and life. These marks of the Christian life signal that a life focused on loving God is a life in tune with what God wants for all of creation as revealed in Scripture. We could say that we are living our lives for God! Our life of faith is focused on a growing relationship with God in Christ shaped by study of the Christian tradition and by serving others. All of these qualities reflect a living faith. In other words, loving God leads to loving words and actions, and others see our faith in the way we live.

It is critically important for us to come to a shared vision of our hopes and expectations for a congregational ministry of making disciples because it will be this vision that guides our planning for this ministry. Sometimes our vision for forming faith might seem an impossible task and we wonder, *How can we help persons grow in love of God and neighbor when we ourselves are trying to grow in faith? How can we prepare ourselves to form faith? How do we help others have the mind of Christ and walk as Christ walked?* Our reassurance comes from knowing that it is God who helps people grow in faith over a lifetime through the work of the Holy Spirit. And so, as we create our own vision for making disciples, we are guided and comforted by the fact that this is not something the church does alone. Rather, the members of the church are participating in God's work. It is God who leads persons to faith and who guides growth in faith.

Thinking, Reflecting, Acting

Reflect and then discuss with others:

What are the characteristics that define a Christian life for you?

What is your vision for a congregational ministry of making disciples?

Making Disciples

Before going any further, we need to pause and consider three important questions, beginning with, *What does it mean to make disciples?* In truth, making disciples, or even forming faith, is not something the church does alone. In some ways, it is misleading to use the phrase "making disciples" to name our ministry because God is the one who makes disciples. It is God who plants the seed of growth in each person. It is God's Spirit within each person that invites that person into a new relationship with God through Jesus Christ. The church is called to participate in God's work of making disciples. I use the word *called* to indicate my belief that this truly is a ministry, a ministry of accompanying others on their pilgrimage in faith. As we consider how to create a ministry of forming faith, it will be important to reflect on what God does and what we, as the church, are called to do on behalf of those who seek authentic relationship, faithful community, and deeper meaning in their lives.

Cultivating a relationship with God and authentic relationships with others in a culture of hospitality invites persons to a pilgrimage in faith. As Christians, we are following our Hebrew ancestors as a pilgrim people. Thomas Groome, religious educator, writes, "We are a pilgrim people in time, coming down through history, moving ever forward toward our 'end time.'"[6] So the word pilgrimage points to the fact that Christian faith formation is a *process over time*. A process is a series of experiences and events designed to achieve our goal, so at the very least we need a vision for the direction of the pilgrim journey. Where are we traveling from? What are we leaving behind? What are we traveling to? What do we need for the journey?

It is unlikely that the faith pilgrim's path will be an uninterrupted straight line to our destination. This process may be a winding path with some dead ends along the way, more like a maze at times than a superhighway. And we may have to build the road as we go, as Nelle Morton observes in her reflection on women's spirituality: "Ordinarily a journey takes us over roads that have been well laid out and well traveled, moving steadily toward a destination. But somehow . . . road-building becomes inseparable from the journey itself."[7] Even if we have to do some road building, we have those who have gone before us pointing the way. So we could also say that this pilgrimage in faith is on a trajectory that begins with those faithful Christians who have traveled the road before us and who lead us into the future toward a deeper relationship with God. Our pilgrimage in faith is a journey built on our trust in a God who provides the pathway of faith through new experiences and insights that lead to authentic relationship, faithful community, and deeper meaning through communion with God and all of creation.

Growing in Faith

As a pilgrim people, the church participates in the pilgrimage of faith by planning ways to support and nurture those who are on the way. Groome writes that "the educators' role is to ensure that the heritage of the past pilgrimage not be lost, but intentionally remembered and made available to the present. And it is equally their role to maintain the ongoingness of the pilgrimage, seeing to it that both the present and its past are a creative and transforming activity toward an open future."[8] Here, Groome is reminding us of the importance of our religious tradition and the idea that our pilgrimage of faith does not end at a certain age or stage but continues as we are drawn ever closer to God. As a result, those who create a ministry of making disciples need to consider a second question, *How do people grow in faith?* A ministry of making disciples involves a project of designing teaching and learning experiences for persons who are traveling the way of faith. The challenge for the church lies in the fact that while each individual's journey in faith has much in common with others, it is also unique.

In an unending curiosity about finding some commonality in how persons grow in faith, Christian educators and psychologists have proposed various theories that serve to inform our ministry.

In 1976, John Westerhoff proposed four stages of faith that define a process of growth beginning with "*experienced faith*," a faith that is nurtured in infancy and continues into early childhood with an experience of primary caregivers as role models for a Christian way of life.[9] It is important that the actions of these models of the Christian life be congruent with their words so that young children develop a sense of trust in their relationships and participate in the religious experience of their caregivers. This idea was asserted even more strongly by Horace Bushnell in 1861 when he addressed the role of parents in Christian nurture and argued that parents should raise their children so "that the child is to grow up a Christian, and never know himself [or herself] as being otherwise."[10] Westerhoff and Bushnell are only two of many theorists who point to the critical responsibility of primary caregivers in nurturing the seeds of faith in infants and young children.

During school, a child's world expands when he or she is exposed to the larger community, particularly school and church. This is the arena of Westerhoff's "*affiliative faith*," a time when children learn the stories of faith and discover what it means to be a member of a faithful community. Children see others trying to follow God's will through the joys and challenges of their lives. As members of the Christian community, children are included in practicing this faithful life. When children move into adolescence and young adulthood, they begin to address questions of faith and identity. In this period of "*searching faith*," young adults are testing their beliefs and trying on alternative perspectives of faith and practice. Their expanded experience in the world raises questions about authentic relationship, and a search for deeper meaning often calls forth service. Growth in faith continues in middle and older adulthood as persons come to an "*owned faith*" in which belief and action are one, as they become living witnesses to what it means to be Christian.[11]

In summary, Westerhoff's theory described the movement from a Christian lifestyle first imposed by external authorities, such as parents or teachers, to an internalized faith that has become assimilated into identity and lifestyle.[12] Westerhoff's proposal is particularly helpful because it draws broad brushstrokes of growing in faith with less danger of judging those who do not fit into more closely defined stages of other theories. It is also important to remember that all four stages of faith are important in every part of a person's pilgrimage in faith, even if persons decide to pursue their desire to find authentic relationship, faithful community, and deeper meaning in adulthood. While Westerhoff's proposal may sound like the pilgrimage ends with owned faith, it does not. Even when persons reach the point of an owned faith, they still need the relationships and experiences of experienced, affiliative, and searching faith as God continues to work in their lives through their deepening relationship with God, self, others, and creation.

Another proposal about how people grow in faith came in 1981 through the research of James Fowler who discussed six more precisely defined "stages of faith" that ranged from early childhood to later adulthood. Fowler adopted Erik Erikson's idea that the development of basic trust in infancy is a critical foundation to his stages of faith development.[13] Building on trusting relationships with early caregivers, Fowler's first stage of faith focuses on the influence of "examples, moods, actions and stories of the visible faith" as faithful adults relate to young children.[14] In the school years, a child's world widens with new experiences and relationships, and they begin to learn the stories of faith for themselves in the second stage of faith.[15] The questioning of adolescents and their expanding arenas of life experience contribute to the development of "identity," "values," and "belief." This is a time of conforming to the norms of a primary group and a time of testing the bounds of authority. Fowler indicates that many adults in the United States remain in this third stage throughout their lives, focused on self and individuality within the context of a primary group.[16] When adults begin to recognize and address the tension between defining oneself and being defined by a group, between being for oneself and being for others, they have moved to the fourth stage of faith.[17] Fowler's fifth stage of faith is one that is defined by a willingness to live in the midst of paradox. It is characterized by ongoing reflection and critique of one's own faith and openness to the truth in the faith of others with a concern for justice.[18] The final stage is more of a vision for Fowler since there are so few who grow into a "universalizing faith." Fowler names people like Gandhi, Martin Luther King, Jr., and Mother Teresa as examples. For me, these are persons who embody the dangerous love of the great commandment. In their love of God and neighbor, they stand against the powers of the world on behalf of the oppressed. As a result, they are seen as subversive and often die for the cause of loving God's creation.[19]

In contrast to using a stage theory to explain how persons grow in faith, Maria Harris and Gabriel Moran argued in 1997 that a theory describing stages for growth in faith is using the wrong "metaphor" for Christian faith formation. They propose that a more appropriate Christian understanding is that "a person develops in relation to wholeness" and grows toward "the communion of all."[20] Although Harris and Moran do not give a precise definition of what they mean by wholeness, both of these ideas— wholeness and communion—reflect the spiritual nature of a pilgrimage in faith and relate to our earlier discussion of the human search for authentic relationship, faithful community, and deeper meaning. Wholeness is centeredness within that comes from being at one with Jesus Christ, an experience of being heard, being known, and being accepted by God and others. Communion is a deep mutual interdependence with God and one another, as well as creation. In other words, growing in a deeper relationship with God and all of creation is to grow toward wholeness and communion.

I concur with Harris and Moran that growth in faith is about growing in relationship with God and others. In 2000, I offered my own proposal for the way persons grow in faith based on the theological assumption that God is the source of love who invites us into an ever-deepening relationship that draws us toward communion with God and one another. Growth in faith begins with God's ever present *invitation to communion*, to a new or renewed relationship with God. We experience this invitation through the work of the Holy Spirit within us. The Spirit awakens us to our need for God in our lives, our need for God's forgiveness, and our desire for a new life that brings us deeper meaning and purpose for our lives. *Deepening communion* is the second phase of our growth in faith as we experience the healing that comes from God's grace. In response to God's love for us, we are able, with God's grace, to turn our lives outward to express our growing love of God by loving our neighbor.[21] It is important to note here that our neighbor is not just the person that we would choose, but every person is our neighbor by virtue of being a child of God. The final phase of this process of growing in faith is *full communion* with God when persons come to love God with all their hearts and minds and souls and they are adopted as children of God.[22] I would describe this ultimately as the coming of the reign of God when all persons are gathered together as brothers and sisters to live in full communion with God and all of God's children. It is this model of growing in faith that I will use throughout the remainder of this book as we consider together what it means to travel the pathway of faith together as a communion of grace, creating an intentional learning and serving community that nourishes lives of faith.

Unlike theories that attach a particular age range to each stage of faith development, my proposal for growing in communion with God visualizes a winding path along which persons move as they are led by God's invitation into deeper relationship. There is an element of readiness and choice involved in the pilgrimage. God invites us, but we have a choice about how we will respond. If we turn away, God's invitation of grace always remains available to us. Once we take our first step, however tentative, toward God in response to God's invitation, we are on our way as God continues to invite us into an ever-deepening relationship. At times, our steps may be halting, and we may stop for a rest along the way. But throughout this process of growing in faith, God's Spirit is at work within us conforming our lives to Christ, and we respond by trying to live more Christ-like lives in response to God's love.

Growing in communion with God and one another on our pilgrimage in faith requires attention to both heart and life—the inner life of faith of loving God and the outer life of loving neighbor. Harris and Moran even go so far as to say that "the inner life has its *necessary* expression in outward activity."[23] From this perspective, we could assume that our service in the world is an embodiment of our inner faith, but we can also see that serving others nurtures our inner life as well. To cultivate this growth in communion with God and others, Harris and Moran indicate that Christian faith formation should include spiritual disciplines that cultivate the inner life *and* "two kinds of outer activity that complement the spiritual disciplines: the study of Christian sources and the performance of Christian service."[24] Here, we once again encounter the importance of an informed and active faith. In partnership with spiritual disciplines such as prayer, worship, and participating in the Lord's Supper, we study Scripture and the history of the church as we seek new ways to serve God in the world. Studying the tradition of the church gives us a window into the faith pilgrimage of all those who preceded us in the tradition of the church—our family's story of faith. Just like us, our ancestral mothers and fathers in faith sought to be faithful. By studying their lives, we gain insight into what it means to love God and neighbor for the time in which we live.

Thinking, Reflecting, Acting

As you think about the ways persons grow in faith, which theory (or combination of theories) discussed above make the most sense for you?

Assemble a small group to research developmental theories from people such as Erik Erikson, Lawrence Kohlberg, Carol Gilligan, James Fowler, Robert Kegan, and Sharon Parks (found in Additional Reading at the end of this chapter). Then discuss the implications for a ministry of forming faith.

Go to www.berghuis.co.nz/abiator/lsi/lsiframe.html to test your own learning style and find descriptions of the ways persons learn. Discuss the results with a friend or your design team and talk about the implications of what you have learned for a congregational ministry of forming faith.

Check your public library, as well as denominational libraries and public television, to see what resources you can find about different age groups in the contemporary context and how they grow in faith. For example, the television documentary "The Merchants of Cool" helps us understand societal and commercial pressures on young people in the United States.

Living and Learning in a Communion of Grace

In this discussion of what is needed for cultivating the heart and life of Christians who are growing in love of God and neighbor, we find the role of the church in a ministry of making disciples. *The church is called to be God's pilgrim people, a communion of grace that nourishes and supports those who seek authentic relationship, faithful community, and deeper meaning in relationship to God and all of creation.* To talk about being a communion of grace is to consider the nature of the church. For the apostle Paul, all of the baptized are one body in Christ (1 Cor 12:13). It is baptism that makes us one even if we come from different backgrounds, cultures, or social status. But being one in Christ does not eliminate diversity. As New Testament scholar Richard Hays writes of 1 Corinthians 12, "In verses 14-20, the major theme is *the necessity of diversity.*"[25] Those who are bound together in one body have distinctive gifts, and this diversity of gifts is necessary in the church. As Hays notes, "Each person should accept gracefully and gratefully whatever gifts God has given and use them for the benefit of the community."[26] This is the communion of grace that is needed to nurture growth in faith, a communion that celebrates and honors diversity in the body of Christ.

But a communion of grace is also characterized by interdependence. After discussing the church as the many baptized into one body and the necessity of sharing diverse gifts in the community, Hays observes that Paul's "focus shifts slightly in verses 21-26 to the *interdependence* of the members of the body."[27] To be one body means that each person's gifts are necessary for the whole, and the members of the body are to care for one another. Regardless of a person's status or gifts, each person is important to the life of the community. Members of the body recognize their need for one another and celebrate the God-given gifts that each person brings to the life of the whole church. This understanding of the church is very different from what the people of Corinth have known as community. In his discussion of Paul's theology, James Dunn writes,

> Paul shifts the corporate image of the Christian community from that of the nation state (historic Israel) to that of body politic, that is, from a community identified by ethnic and traditional boundary markers to one whose members are drawn from different nationalities and social strata and whose prosperity depends on their mutual cooperation and their working harmoniously together.[28]

Dunn is reminding us that just as diverse gifts are necessary for the body of Christ, so is the understanding that we are one body in our life together, a communion.

A contemporary image for our life together comes from theologian Jürgen Moltmann's discussion of the Trinity and how we find a "home in God" through communion with God. Moltmann characterizes the relationship of the three persons of the Trinity as "mutual indwelling" so that there is "mutuality without mixing or separating."[29] In other words, there is interdependence and diversity in the communion of the Trinity. The way the persons of the Trinity live in communion is a pattern for how we are to live in communion with God and one another. Mutual indwelling points to a degree of interdependence and caring for one another that many of us seek. While our faith community will never be one as God is One, with God's help we can create a communion that cultivates living together in love. The phrase "mutuality without mixing or separating" also points to the importance of diversity.

Moltmann writes that the persons of the Trinity give "one another open life-space for their mutual indwelling."[30] As the church practices mutual indwelling, the members share common commitments to faith and a concern for the well-being of each member. In open life-space, or "room-giving," the church provides opportunities for sharing diverse gifts in its ministry and mission.[31] The point is that we can be interdependent and still give each other space for difference through room-giving. The value of Paul's theology and Moltmann's proposal for being a communion of grace is that they tell us that we do not all have to be alike. In fact, it is critically important that we are not. A communion of grace that is mutually indwelling and room-giving welcomes diversity. So as we think about living in a communion of grace, we need to find ways to cultivate the interdependence of mutual indwelling and the room-giving of offering open space for others to grow in their own unique God-given ways.

Realizing that a communion of grace participates in God's work of forming faith brings us to a third question for our consideration: *How do we grow together as a communion of grace?* It has become apparent that ongoing growth in faith requires participation in the life of the church because it is only in relationship with other faithful Christians that persons grow in love of God and neighbor. Since growth in faith is both individual and communal, the church needs to be creative and intentional about its role in forming faith, beginning with an understanding of what it means to be a communion of grace. Several critical assumptions guide our planning.

A communion of grace is built on God's love and welcomes all. We have already discussed the fact that it is God's great love for creation that invites us into a deepening relationship with God. God gives us our community and invites us to travel the journey of faith together. What has been assumed, but not yet explicitly stated, is that there is no limit to God's abundant grace. God loves every part of creation, including every person on this planet. And God's grace is available to each one. When God became human and walked among us, we learned this lesson of God's love for creation. Story after story in the Bible tells us of Jesus' love for the outcast, those that others scorned or ignored. As we saw in Jesus' encounter with the Samaritan woman, his willingness to reach across racial/ethnic, religious, and gender lines to listen was the beginning of trust and an invitation to new relationship so that the woman's life could be transformed. This opportunity for new life is always available to us through God's grace, and with Jesus' death and resurrection came the assurance that nothing we are or say or do separates us from God's love.

Our response to God's abundant grace is to practice a Christian way of life as individuals and as congregations, so that others might experience God's abundant grace through us. In other words, we open ourselves to become what I have previously called "a vehicle of God's grace for others" as God uses our lives for the transformation of others.[32] Opening our lives to a deepening relationship with God and to our neighbor makes us available for God's purposes. This same openness to God and neighbor becomes the foundation of a communion of grace. In other words, God's grace calls us to a ministry of hospitality, to welcoming the stranger in others, as well as in ourselves, into our midst. Eric Law calls this "inclusion . . . a discipline of extending our boundary to take into consideration another's needs, interests, experience, and perspective, which will lead to clearer understanding of ourselves and others, fuller description of the issue at hand, and possibly a newly negotiated boundary of the community to which we belong."[33] This kind of hospitality involves both risk and promise as we extend our boundaries to consider the needs and interests of others. The risk is in making ourselves vulnerable in welcoming others into our midst. The promise is in the hope of growing in communion with God through sharing our lives together.

Once again we need to remember that we do not do this on our own. It is God's abundant grace that helps us extend the boundaries of our faith communities to include those who are different from ourselves. In a creative design for helping congregations move to inclusion, Law suggests a model that helps people move out of their "safe zone" by creating a "grace margin," a space persons enter together to explore shared commitments and differences.[34] This model helps us create a safe place where persons can share faith and life, where they can learn together.

One of the questions that emerges in growing as a communion of grace open to the diversity of others is, How can we grow together if we have different backgrounds and come from different ways of life? *We know that a congregational ministry of making disciples in a diverse community will undoubtedly call upon us to be open to hearing others in new ways, so we need to find the willingness in ourselves to live with ambiguity, conflict, and compromise.*[35] This diversity is essential to our life together in a communion of grace. In his commentary on First Corinthians, Hays observes, "Because God has arranged the body as an interdependent organism in which diversity is essential, the differences between the members should not lead to division . . . but to the members' caring for one another (v. 25)."[36] Hospitality, inclusion, open life-space, caring, loving God and loving neighbor are signs that a communion of grace is growing in communion with God and one another.

A communion of grace nurtures relationships with God and one another. If we choose to move fully into the intentional life of a communion of grace, it is God's abundant grace that guides our growth in the interdependence of mutual indwelling and the grace of room-giving. In chapter 1, we learned that authentic relationship and the creation of a community of grace begins with hearing. If persons find a place to be heard in the church, they will discover authentic relationship, faithful community, and deeper meaning for their lives. This is a foundation for forming faith, so an integral part of learning in a communion of grace is creating opportunities for persons to hear one another. These opportunities are present any time there is open life-space for persons to share with one another in settings such as structured study groups, prayer groups, fellowship gatherings, parenting groups, or mission ventures. Any time and anywhere that people gather in the name of Christ, there is the possibility of growing in communion by nurturing relationships. An intentionality of purpose is needed here, and the fourth chapter will offer ideas for relationships, structures, and practices that cultivate love of God and neighbor.

A communion of grace focuses on living and learning. Dedication to cultivating the inner life of faith and the outer life of study and service shapes a ministry of forming the heart and life of Christian disciples. As pilgrims, we find deeper meaning for our lives through developing our practice of spiritual disciplines, studying our inheritance from the Christian tradition, being instructed in the ways of faith, practicing mutual care, participating in Christian fellowship, practicing a Christian life, and serving our neighbor. This focus on spiritual disciplines, learning, and living is how the church participates in God's work of nurturing persons in faith. The role of a communion of grace is to accompany one another as pilgrims in faith because we are all on the pathway of faith—some are walking ahead, some beside, and some are yet to come. A congregation that focuses on persons' growing in heart and life—the inner and outer lives of faith—also cultivates the life of the faith community. And a ministry of forming faith extends throughout the whole week to nurture faithful living in daily life. In other words, the church is a group of persons who are journeying together in faith toward deeper communion with God and one another.

Finally, *a communion of grace expects transformation*. If we believe that God draws us into relationship through invitation to communion, deepening communion, and full communion with God, then we expect transformation—transformation from brokenness to wholeness, from questioning faith to informed faith, from community to communion. Expecting transformation is a matter of faith, believing that God has the power to make all things new. Through transformation, a faith community grows into a communion of grace, and God's Spirit draws the members of the church into ever-deepening relationships with God and one another. In these relationships, persons find new identity in communion as they share their common vocation of loving God and neighbor.

Thinking, Reflecting, Acting

Share what living in a communion of grace means to you by using music, poetry, various art forms.

What is your interpretation of *mutual indwelling* and *room-giving*? Where do you see these characteristics of communion at work in your congregation?

Toward Creating a Congregational Ministry of Making Disciples

FORMING FAITH IN A COMMUNION OF GRACE

Discuss the main ideas of this chapter with your planning team for a congregational ministry of making disciples. What insights have you gained? What questions do you have?

Vision and Goal

A person is Christian in heart and life.
Marks of a Christian:

- Scripture is the only and sufficient rule for daily life.
- Faith is more than opinion—need knowledge and understanding, study and reflection, active discussion.
- Do good; avoid doing harm to ourselves, others, and creation.
- Love God by loving neighbor.

Making Disciples

What does it mean to make disciples?

- God plants the seed and invites persons to new relationship.
- The church participates in God's work, a ministry of accompanying others on their pilgrimage in faith.
- Pilgrimage: Christian faith formation is a process over time.

How do persons grow in faith?

- Westerhoff: *experienced faith, affiliative faith, searching faith, owned faith*
- Fowler: stages of faith from childhood to adulthood—trusting relationships to dangerous love of universalizing faith
- Harris and Moran: *developing wholeness and growing in communion of all*; cultivating the inner life of faith through spiritual disciplines; the outer life of faith through study of the Christian tradition and service

❧ Matthaei: God's *invitation to communion*; God's healing grace and our expression of love of God through love of neighbor in *deepening communion*; adopted as children of God in *full communion* with God and all of creation

How does the church grow as a communion of grace?

❧ The church as God's pilgrim people is one body in Christ growing together in faith.

🕊 Interdependence of communion—mutual indwelling

🕊 Necessity of diversity in the body—room-giving

❧ A communion of grace is built on God's love and welcomes all.

❧ A communion of grace nurtures relationships with God and each other.

❧ A communion of grace focuses on learning and living.

❧ A communion of grace expects transformation.

Other Suggestions for Reflecting and Planning

These suggestions can be used for individual reflection, for discussion in a Christian education event for youth or adults, or for sharing with a team who is designing a congregational ministry of making disciples.

1. Discuss this question together: For what purpose do we make disciples?[37]

2. Write out your aim and goals for a congregational ministry of making disciples. What is it you want to accomplish in the next year? the next five years? the next ten years?

3. Discuss God's work in forming faith. What does the church do to participate in God's work of forming faith?

4. Read Eric Law's *Inclusion: Making Room for Grace* and establish a "grace margin" in your church.

5. Think about how you could "do" each of these steps in building a communion of grace. What relationships or activities would

help your congregation grow in these ways? Assess the strengths and areas for development of these steps:

STEPS IN BUILDING COMMUNION	AREAS OF STRENGTH	IDEAS FOR DEVELOPMENT
Keep our eyes fixed on God, take on the mind of Christ		
Consider your shared life together. Do you have a shared vision, goals, expectations, and mission?		
Create an interconnected and focused ministry of forming faith. What persons and groups share in the task of making disciples? What groups in the church need to be included?		
How do you prepare teachers, leaders, and pastoral staff to participate in forming faith in a communion of grace?		
When and how is your ministry shaped by the sacraments?		
Where do you see the characteristics of communion discussed in this chapter?		

6. Further assess the diversity in your congregational life:

AREA OF CONGREGATIONAL LIFE	AREAS OF STRENGTH	IDEAS FOR DEVELOPMENT
Wrestling with ideas— opportunity to share different perspectives without judgment		
Relationships —Hospitality for all kinds of neighbors —open to getting to know persons from different cultures and ways of life		
Leadership—a variety of persons of various ages providing leadership throughout the church's life		
Activities—willing to participate in activities that reflect different cultures and ways of life		

Additional Reading for This Chapter

Erikson, Erik H. *The Life Cycle Completed*. New York: W.W. Norton, 1982.

Fowler, James. *Becoming Adult, Becoming Christian: Adult Development and Christian Faith*. San Francisco: Jossey-Bass, 2000.

Gilligan, Carol, Janie Victoria Ward, and Jill McLean Taylor, eds. *Mapping the Moral Domain*. Cambridge, Mass.: Harvard University Press, 1988.

Harris, Maria and Gabriel Moran, "Educating Persons." Pages 58–73 in *Mapping Christian Education: Approaches to Congregational Learning*. Edited by Jack L. Seymour. Nashville: Abingdon Press, 1997.

Kegan, Robert. *The Evolving Self: Problem and Process in Human Development*. Cambridge, Mass.: Harvard University Press, 1982.

Eric Law, *Inclusion: Making Room for Grace* (St. Louis: Chalice Press, 2000).

Parks, Sharon Daloz. *Big Questions, Worthy Dreams: Mentoring Young Adults in Their Search for Meaning, Purpose, and Faith.* San Francisco: Jossey-Bass, 2000.

Webb-Mitchell, Brett. "Leaving Development Behind and Beginning Pilgrimage." *Religious Education* 96, no. 1 (Winter 2001).

CHAPTER THREE

Following in the Steps of Love

A dispute also arose among them as to which one of them was to be regarded
as the greatest. But [Jesus] said to them, "The kings of the Gentiles lord it
over them; and those in authority over them are called benefactors. But not
so with you; rather the greatest among you must become like the youngest,
and the leader like one who serves. For who is greater, the one who is at the
table or the one who serves?" (Luke 22:24-27)

I grew up in the age of the great movie musicals—*South Pacific, Oklahoma, The Sound of Music, Carousel, The King and I,* and *Annie Get Your Gun* to name a few. They filled my head with music and shaped my worldview to the extent that I came to the unrealistic expectation (since corrected) that evil will be overcome and everyone will live happily ever after. So it was no surprise that a song came floating into my consciousness as I thought about the disciples' dispute about greatness—a signature song from *Annie Get Your Gun:* "Anything you can do, I can do better."

The question of who is the greatest seems to be part of the human condition that most of us cannot escape in the United States. We constantly compare ourselves to others and make judgments about each other in a way that reflects a competitive individualistic perspective on the world with little sense of the importance of all of the parts of a whole, particularly the parts that represent different cultures and different ways of life from our own. Unfortunately, this type of dispute is also common in our local churches. We find ourselves enmeshed in conflicts over divided priorities that sometimes polarize our communities of faith. In one church, these symptoms were evident in a developing youth ministry when the youth and youth leaders were in conflict with the finance committee who did not want to approve funds for the ministry, the trustees who did not want a physical space "downgraded" to a youth gathering area, and an adult class who did not want to leave "their" space. This conflict pointed to a lack of shared vision and goals—and an unwillingness to listen. While the competitive spirit sometimes provides motivation for us to develop our God-given gifts, it can also hamper the creation of the communion needed for forming faith, a communion based on authentic relationship, the interdependence of a faithful people, and the discovery of deeper meaning in relationship to God.

Leadership is a critical issue for a communion of grace seeking to create a congregational ministry of making disciples. What type of leadership is needed for a pilgrim people traveling and learning together in faith? What are the tasks of leadership? If we want the mission and ministry of our congregational life to be effective in making disciples, then we need to explore the role of leaders in forming faith. To this end, we turn to Luke's account of the Passover meal that teaches us about leaders who follow Christ's servant ministry in the steps of love.

The Dispute Over Leadership

Luke sets the scene for the dramatic climax to the gospel story of Jesus' life and ministry. Jesus and the disciples were gathered in the upper room for the Passover feast when Jesus announced that one would betray him. After the disciples dispute which one would betray him, they turn in the very next verse to ask which is the greatest.[1] Who will be the greatest leader of them all?

In the face of the dispute, Jesus says to the disciples "The rulers of the Gentiles lord it over them; and those in authority over them are called benefactors. But not so with you; rather the greatest among you must become like the youngest, and the leader like one who serves" (vv. 25-26). Luke is reminding the reader that Jesus has previously warned his disciples not to become full of self-importance following "the behavior patterns of the Pharisees and scribes (12:1; 20:46)."[2] And before going to Jerusalem, Jesus had even brought a child into their midst saying "the least among all of you is the greatest" (9:26-28).[3] But here, at the Passover meal, the lessons have been forgotten so Jesus offers an alternative vision of what it means to be a leader—one who serves. Jesus takes on the role of the poor to serve the meal and asks, "For who is greater, the one who is at the table or the one who serves?" (v. 27). With this action and by these words, Jesus turns the image of leadership upside down. Author Joel Green writes that "Jesus is not teaching that his followers cannot be rulers or benefactors, but that their manner of ruling and benefaction must be utterly transformed. According to Jesus, disciples are, like God, to give without expectation of return."[4]

This is the model of servant ministry needed for a congregational ministry of making disciples. Pilgrim people who follow Jesus in the steps of love become the role models and what I have called "faith mentors," those "who, as living representatives of God's grace, participate in the relational, vocational, and spiritual growth of others" on a pilgrimage of faith.[5] What follows is a proposal for how all of God's people participate in a ministry of serving throughout the life of the church and in the wider community.

Thinking, Reflecting, Acting

If you take this passage from the Gospel of Luke seriously, what is the biggest challenge for leadership in your local congregation?

What would need to change, and how would you go about it?

A Shared Ministry of Serving—Diakonia

Jesus' own life and work provided such a unique model of servant ministry that a new name emerged for it.[6] New Testament scholar Eduard Schweizer says it is remarkable that instead of choosing one of the more common Greek terms for defining "official" ministry such as *telos*, *timē*, *archē*, or *leitourgia*, the New Testament writers chose a rarely-used Greek word, *diakonia*.[7] The biblical writers' reason for this choice offers an important principle in understanding the servant ministry of the whole church. In Schweizer's words:

> This spontaneous usage [of *diakonia*] in all the different layers of [New Testament] literature shows what an impression the challenge of Jesus' way of life and teaching made on all his followers. The total (eschatological) newness of *a service without institutional hierarchies or resort to force was so striking that it became impossible to speak of the honor or the exemplary model of an "official" ministry apart from that of any other person in the church.* Wherever somebody was serving Christ, it was exactly what a slave would do for his lord, i.e., a simple, worldly service, not a domination of others.[8]

Note that the emphasis in the New Testament is on *service without hierarchies* to the extent that everyone who served Christ was honored, not just those in official ministry. In other words, the writers in the early church understood that following in Jesus' steps of love meant that servant ministry is a *nonhierarchical partnership* of all the people of God. All those who served Christ were in partnership to carry out the church's mission of loving God and serving neighbor.

A second image for servant ministry that I find helpful is that of "go-between." Warren Carter, another New Testament scholar, writes that "*diakonos* in Luke's usage typically designates a commissioned spokesperson or agent, a 'go-between' who ministers of behalf of God or the Christian community."[9] In other words, all of God's people are called to a go-between ministry of service, and this mutual ministry of following in the steps of Jesus expresses itself then as a *nonhierarchical partnership of go-betweens on behalf of God and the Christian community.*

Laity and the ministry of serving.[10] I believe that all baptized Christians are called to servant ministry by virtue of their baptism.

Baptism is more than an individual experience; it incorporates persons into a community of faith formed by God's grace and called to serve God in the world. Through the baptismal covenant, God brings into being what author and educator Gayle Carlton Felton calls a "servant community," a community whose members serve as representatives of God's love and saving grace in the world through servant ministry.[11] This means that all Christians are called to love God and the world that God has created by serving their neighbor.

In reality, baptism establishes an order of servant ministry by creating a covenant community that supports and cares for its members while holding them accountable for their role as servants of Christ in the world. This is "the ministry of all Christians":

> The heart of Christian ministry is Christ's ministry of out-reaching love. Christian ministry is the expression of the mind and mission of Christ by a community of Christians that demonstrates a common life of gratitude and devotion, witness and service, celebration and discipleship. All Christians are called through their baptism to this ministry of servanthood in the world to the glory of God and for human fulfillment. The forms of this ministry are diverse in locale, in interest, and in denominational accent, yet always catholic in spirit and outreach.[12]

Taking on the mind and mission of Christ through servant ministry occurs in a variety of ways and places. Through servant ministry, the members of the church witness to the life-giving power of God's saving grace and invite others into the church's communion to grow in love of God and neighbor. In other words, the pilgrim people share their God-given gifts through the church's mission and ministry of representing God's love and saving grace in the world through servant ministry. And this is not only a "Sunday ministry" or "mission ministry," it is an "everyday ministry." In every place Christians walk, they are servant ministers, go-betweens on behalf of God and the Christian community.

To talk about the critical importance of the servant ministry of all Christians as a nonhierarchical partnership of go-betweens on behalf of God and the Christian community raises a crucial question: If all Christians are called to servant ministry, then what does it mean when some denominations *ordain* persons to serve? In the discussion that follows, you will see that I believe that the ordained are called out from all the people of God to a lifetime of servant leadership as go-betweens on behalf of God and the Christian community and then sent out to lead the members of the church as they continue Christ's servant ministry in the world. In other words, deacons and priests or elders help build up the body of Christ and lead the church in its servant ministry. What makes the servant ministry of the ordained deacon, elder, or priest *distinctive* from the servant ministry of all Christians is the particular kind of servant leadership and go-between activities in their servant leadership. And each form of servant ministry is critically important to the whole—many members in one body.

Since we often assume that ministry is something that only pastors do and because the nature and tasks of ordained ministry are under discussion in several Protestant denominations, I am proposing that we come to a totally different understanding of ministry. *We need to support a shared ministry of serving in which each person has an important role regardless of "rank."* This proposal mirrors the New Testament understanding of servant ministry in that it is a nonhierarchical partnership of persons who are called to do God's work in the world. As a way to highlight the importance of all forms of ministry, I have already discussed the nature and tasks of the laity in servant ministry. Now I turn to the distinctive nature and tasks of the ministry of deacon and elder before bringing the whole picture together.

Deacons and the ministry of serving. Ordained deacons constitute another order of servant ministry. The distinctive servant ministry of the deacon, as expressed in the Episcopalian liturgy, is ordination to a "focused expression"[13] of serving "all people, particularly the poor, the weak, the sick, and the lonely."[14] This statement reflects the go-between nature of the particular ministry of deacon in relation to the poor and oppressed that is common in other Protestant traditions as well. We find this understanding of the deacon's role reflected in 2 Corinthians

(3:6) where Paul's self-identification as a "[minister] of a new covenant" (*diakonos*) provides insight into several aspects of the nature and task of a deacon's go-between ministry. Commentator Victor Paul Furnish wrote that as *diakonos*, Paul is on an "errand" on behalf of God, representing "the redemptive work of Christ" in the church and the world and seeking nothing less than the "reconciliation of humanity to God."[15] Significantly, Paul explicitly connects the go-between ministry of the deacon with the activities of caring for the poor (2 Cor 8:4). And Paul does not claim credit for the success of his ministry on behalf of the poor but describes it as an act of divine grace (2 Cor 8:1).[16] Through his words, Paul reminds us that those who are sent on errands on behalf of God know that it is God's grace that provides all that is needed for the journey.

In this form of servant ministry, the deacon is ordained to serve the community *and* the congregation, connecting the needs of the world with the gifts of God's pilgrim people. In other words, the servant ministry of the deacon attends to *the intersection of the world and the church*. Thus, the distinctive servant ministry of the deacon *embodies* and re-presents the love of God by following Jesus Christ and serving the poor and oppressed in the world.[17] Through personal spiritual life and a ministry of service, the deacon becomes a "life pattern" of what it means to walk in the steps of love through concern for all of God's creation, particularly the poor and oppressed.[18] So the ordained deacon is on an errand for God and the church to minister in the intersection between the community and the church, leading the pilgrim people of God in the same servant ministry. What makes this ministry distinctive is that ordained deacons are called to use their God-given gifts to build a ministry of compassion and justice to the community and to the congregation. The deacon continues the church's tradition of servant ministry with those on the margins and stands in the midst and beside all of God's people in their shared servant ministry in the world.

Deacons are also called to "articulate" a vision for participation in Christ's servant ministry and to challenge God's pilgrim people to love their neighbor in the intersection of the community and the church.[19] In these go-between activities, British Methodist Kenneth Howcroft argues that the deacon "offers a prophetic voice from the margins," sharing the good news of God's love and saving grace through servant ministry in the community and in the church.[20] This prophetic word calls the people of God to be faithful followers of Jesus Christ through servant ministry. And finally, by embodying servant ministry and through preaching and teaching, the deacon is to build up and "lead [all of the people] of God in its servant ministry," equipping the members of the church for carrying out God's errands of mercy and justice in the world.[21]

Elder or priest and the ministry of serving. In another order of servant ministry, the distinctive ministry of the elder or priest is ordination to a focused expression of spiritual leadership and pastoral oversight that prepares the people of God for servant ministry in the world. Spiritual leadership and pastoral oversight are the go-between activities at the heart of the servant ministry of the elder or priest. Howcroft writes that through preaching, by presiding at the sacraments, and by pastoral oversight, elders "are authorised by the Conference to be public people who represent God-in-Christ and the community of the Church in the world . . . as they seek to serve the needs of the Kingdom in the power of the Spirit."[22] Elders and priests are not just public representatives of servant ministry; they also share in servant ministry and provide leadership for the servant ministry of the pilgrim people.

In this form of servant ministry, the elder or priest is on an errand for God and the church to *lead God's pilgrim people in worship and prayer*, embodying the love of God and lifting up the "presence and activity of God-in-Christ in the church and in the world."[23] Through the articulation of the story of faith in preaching, the elder or priest reminds all of the people of God who they are and whose they are and challenges them to use their God-given gifts in a Christian vocation of servant ministry. Loving our neighbor through servant ministry is an expression of our love for God. Through Word and Sacrament, the pilgrim people are reminded of God's love and grace and are prepared for this witness and service in the world. What makes this ministry distinctive is that ordained elders and priests are called to use their God-given gifts to build a community of compassion and justice to fulfill God's mission in the world.

As living representatives of God's love for all creation, elders or priests also become vehicles of God's saving grace as the Spirit works in them to invite others to follow Christ into servant ministry. The elder's role in *leading persons to faith in Jesus Christ* serves God's purpose for the healing of all creation. In this way, the ordained priest or elder continues Christ's ministry of inviting persons into the communion of the church and nurturing their faithful discipleship as they grow in love of God and neighbor. This means that elders or priests need to *claim their teaching authority* by leading studies of Scripture and the Christian tradition so that members of the congregation have knowledge and understanding of the meaning of the Christian life. According to Thomas Frank, these leaders also help the people of God "discern their vocation and use their gifts to fulfill their particular ministries."[24] In other words, the elder cares for the members of the congregation, preparing and organizing them for witness and service in the world, through *exercising pastoral supervision in the congregation*. Finally, the elder leads the Church in *obedience to God's mission in the world*, focusing on the call to the church to participate in God's coming reign by loving all of God's creation and standing against injustice.

Jesus and the ministry of serving. Jesus is the mandate and model for each of these orders of servant ministry—for all Christians who are called and sent on an errand for God to become witnesses of God's love and saving grace through a ministry of serving. In his discussion of Mark 10:45 ("For the Son of Man came not to be served but to serve, and to give his life a ransom for many"), author John Collins argues that Jesus is the Word from which our mandate to serve comes and emphasizes the connection between Word and Service.[25] This point identifies Jesus Christ as a triune "go-between" who offers God's grace to each person, an agent of the communion of the Trinity and the Word who forever joins Word and service in servant ministry. From the table to the streets, Jesus Christ's radical act of love provides for our salvation and witnesses to the ultimate meaning of servant ministry through love of God and neighbor.

To follow in Jesus' steps of love is the ministry of *diakonia*. This means that every current and future form of ministry is needed for carrying on Christ's mission in the world! This ministry is a spiritual partnership of all the people of God bound together in a servant community established at our baptism. Servant ministry is a nonhierarchical partnership in which the Holy Spirit continues to call us to share Christ's ministry as we grow into ever-deepening expressions of love for God and neighbor. Servant ministers are called by God to discover and use their gifts in a Christian vocation of loving God and neighbor. As love of God deepens, the witness of the Spirit through a shared ministry of serving becomes evident in ever-deepening forms of prophetic witness to the community and the church in the go-between activities of servant ministry.

Thinking, Reflecting, Acting

What are the strengths of this argument about servant ministry?

What are the weaknesses of this argument about servant ministry?

If you took this argument seriously, what would change in your congregational life?

A Communion of Servant Leaders

You may be wondering at this point why I have spent this much time and space writing about the shared servant ministry of all the people of the church. My *intention is to propose a different way of being in the church as the heart of a congregational ministry of making disciples, and this requires a major transformation of perspective about leadership.* Rather than assuming that the role of the ordained elder or priest is the greatest and most responsible for ministry, or that our area of particular interest in the church's life is more important than the other areas of congregational life, I am challenging the reader to take the New Testament understanding of *diakonia* seriously. We need to understand that all of God's people and their diverse areas of commitment and interest make up a communion of servant leaders in a communion of grace. We need to see servant ministry as a nonhierarchical partnership of go-betweens on behalf of God and the Christian community. Every member of God's pilgrim people is sent by God on an errand to love God's creation. No one form of ministry or area of the church's life is more important than another. All of these ministries are needed in order for the servant ministry of the church to be fulfilled, so that we take on the mind and mission of Christ to love God's world. If we are serious about a congregational ministry of making disciples, we need to leave our competitive spirit behind and cultivate the expectation that every Christian has a vocation in a shared servant ministry and that each person has the capacity for a role in servant leadership.

This discussion brings us back to the Gospel of Luke and the question of why Luke records the dispute over leadership immediately after the dispute over who will betray Jesus. Green suggests that Luke may be telling us that there is more than one way to betray Jesus and God's kingdom.[26] Rather than spending our time disputing who is the greatest, Luke's Gospel challenges us all to walk together following Jesus Christ's steps of love in a ministry partnership of serving God and neighbor.

This discussion of servant ministry raises the question of how persons both serve and lead and how servant leadership contributes to a congregational ministry of forming faith. I am arguing that it takes a communion of servant leaders to participate in God's work of making faithful disciples who follow in Jesus' steps of love. In a classic resource on servant leadership, Robert Greenleaf shared how his first insights about servant leadership came from Hermann Hesse's *Journey to the East*:

> But to me, this story clearly says that *the great leader is seen as servant first*, and that simple fact is the key to his greatness. Leo

51

was actually the leader all of the time, but he was servant first because that was what he was, *deep down inside*. Leadership was bestowed upon a man who was by nature a servant. It was something given, or assumed, that could be taken away. His servant nature was the real man, not bestowed, not assumed, and not to be taken away. He was servant first.[27]

Greenleaf is arguing that a servant nature is part of one's being while leadership is acquired or bestowed. For Greenleaf, then, servant ministry begins with an inner quality of one's own being. In Greenleaf's words, "The servant-leader *is* servant first. . . . It begins with the natural feeling that one wants to serve, to serve *first*. Then conscious choice brings one to aspire to lead."[28] A servant leader comes to life seeking what there is to share and give rather than what there is to take.

It might be an easier step to think about ourselves as participating in a shared ministry of serving than to see ourselves participating in a communion of servant leaders, since we often think of leaders as those who are "out front," organized, confident, and so on. An online dictionary states that a leader is "a person who rules or guides or inspires others."[29] We can use this definition to propose that for those who are on errands for God in the world, every baptized Christian functions as a servant leader in at least one of these three ways: ruling, guiding, or inspiring. For example, there are those who serve by using their gifts in the governance structures of our congregations or in community organizations. Others may have particular gifts for servant leadership as guides in teaching or in mission ministry. And others are servant leaders, like my high school teacher Mrs. Anderson, who inspire others by the way they live their lives.

The communion of servant leaders is at the heart of a congregational ministry of making disciples. So what is our role in forming faith as a communion of servant leaders? One way to discern our part in making disciples is by considering these questions: How would we describe the servant leaders we have known? What qualities and characteristics made them significant in our lives? How did they help us find authentic relationship, faithful communion, and deeper meaning for our lives as we grew in faith? What gifts do we have that we could share? In my own research on influential relationships, the most frequently mentioned characteristics of persons I now call "faith mentors" were *caring* and *accepting*, two terms that describe a person's awareness of and concern for others, as well as an openness and trustworthiness that contributed to the growth and well-being of others. In other words, we could say that a servant leader knows who we are, cares about our well-being, and provides "a caring and accepting environment for the relationship."[30] It is clear in this research from the late 1980s that authentic relationship, faithful community, and deeper meaning were important to pilgrims in faith then as well as now.

A second characteristic of influential persons from my research was one of pointing the way ahead on one's life pilgrimage through "guidance in shared decision making" and in "development [of] skills for problem solving, analyzing situations, and seeing alternatives."[31] For servant leaders, this characteristic means they are guides for those on a pilgrimage of faith, helping others find their way. Greenleaf also includes this characteristic as a mark for servant leaders when he says they "are better than most at pointing the direction. As long as one is leading, one always has a goal. It may be a goal arrived at by group consensus, or the leader, acting on inspiration, may simply have said, 'Let's go this way.' But the leader always knows what it is and can articulate it for any who are unsure."[32] These insights point to a servant leader who has a vision and a sense of the goal ahead but who is also willing to travel beside others as a pilgrim people.

Another quality of servant leaders is that they listen. As Greenleaf writes, "only a true natural servant automatically responds to any problem by listening *first*. . . . true listening builds strength in other people."[33] We have already discovered the truth of Greenleaf's assertion in our consideration in the first chapter of how hearing and listening begin authentic relationship, build faithful community, transform community into communion, and nurture deeper meaning. But Greenleaf also reminds us that "acceptance of the person . . . requires a tolerance of imperfection."[34] This reminder should not be taken lightly since many of us who are participants in congregational life have unrealistically high expectations for ourselves and others and may only want to include others like ourselves in the communion of the church.

This leads us to a final characteristic for this discussion that the servant leader is a person of faith, one who has faith in God's love and grace, faith in God's care for creation, and faith that God will use the servant leader's life for the transformation of others. A servant leader has a vision of what it means to live in a communion of grace, loving God and loving neighbor. This means that a servant leader goes forth in faith and humility, relying on God's grace to transform lives.

Thinking, Reflecting, Acting

Where do you find a competitive spirit in yourself and in your congregation over the ministry of your church?

What characteristics would you name for servant leaders?

What gifts do you bring to servant ministry?

Where can you provide servant leadership?

Tasks of Servant Ministry

In our reflection, we have claimed that at baptism we are all called to participate in a shared ministry of servant leadership as those who follow in Christ's steps of love. We have learned that servant ministry in a communion of grace is a nonhierarchical partnership of go-betweens on behalf of God and the Christian community. Therefore every Christian is to take on the mind of Christ and use her or his God-given gifts through a variety of servant leadership roles to love God and serve neighbor. To follow our tongue-in-cheek musical theme, we need to change our tune from "Anything you can do, I can do better" to "All who follow Jesus, all around the world! *Yes, we're the church together!*"[35] In light of the call to follow in Jesus' steps of love, I propose the following tasks for the communion of servant leaders in a congregational ministry of making disciples. These tasks are based on insights from the interaction between Jesus and the Samaritan woman discussed in chapter 2.

Making connections. We have seen in the first two chapters that being heard, being known, and being accepted are the basic elements of authentic relationship. Just as Jesus first spoke to the Samaritan woman, thereby recognizing her as a person of value, all servant leaders have the capacity to follow Jesus' lead. Speaking to or smiling at those who might pass by unseen whether they are children, shy or introverted persons, or those who are different from ourselves in race, ethnicity, or class is the first step in establishing connections that lead to a trusting relationship.

In fact making connections can happen without even speaking. A number of years ago I was teaching a class in clown ministry, a ministry that has honoring and valuing people as its aim. Clown ministers might play jokes on themselves but never on others. At the end of the class, I took my student clowns to visit a local nursing home with instructions to ask permission to enter the rooms and to listen well. As I wandered through the halls looking in on the students visiting the residents, I noticed that one student was spending the entire visit sitting quietly by an elderly woman. The student's face reflected an attitude of compassionate listening with the heart as the bedridden woman talked quietly through the whole visit. During our reflection time with the nursing home chaplain, we learned that this woman had not spoken to anyone for over two months. By listening with love, the student clown had heard this woman to speech and she had found authentic relationship, faithful community, and deeper meaning in the process. This experience taught me that being intentional about making connections as one walks in the steps of love, has a significant impact on persons who are growing in faith at any of life's stages.

Engaging the story.[36] Hearing a person's story with our ears and listening with our hearts creates the space for persons to find their own voices. Just as Jesus listened deeply to the Samaritan woman, recognizing the pain of her life, servant leaders *listen to the stories* of those who are searching for faith in their lives. This is the first step in engaging the story.

A second step is *drawing out questions of faith* as Jesus did when he and the Samaritan woman talked about the meaning of faith. I think this step may be particularly difficult for church people for a couple of reasons. My experience of interviewing previously churched people and churched people for my dissertation research taught me that church people sometimes feel that asking hard questions is being unfaithful. In fact, several of the previously churched people, including Maria, Amelia, and Mai discussed in chapter 1, said they left the church because they felt their questions were not welcome. Another reason that we may find drawing out questions a difficult task is our own sense of insecurity in the faith. We are afraid of not having the answers. But we need to remember that a pilgrimage in faith is about searching and finding our way as we follow God's will for our lives. It is not just about right answers. It is about asking questions to discern meaning, and this is something that servant leaders share with those who are seeking to grow in faith.

We now know from our reflection to this point that one mark of a Christian is to have knowledge and understanding of the faith tradition, and there is no way we can come to that understanding without asking the questions that challenge us. God's truth comes to us through wrestling with the meaning of faith in the company of other pilgrims on the way. So a third step in engaging the story is *entering into honest conversation* using some basic ground rules for discussion such as Eric Law's "respectful community guidelines" so that the conversation does not turn into whose idea is right or the greatest.[37] The idea here is for servant leaders to help persons learn to listen to others, trying to understand their perspective and why they believe what they do. There is also an opportunity for servant leaders to bring God's Story into the discussion as a way of connecting God's Story with each person's story.[38] Honest conversation about the intersection of these stories allows participants, including servant leaders, to wrestle with questions of faith, trusting that God is a participant in the conversation.

Coming to a shared vision. In her interaction with Jesus, the Samaritan woman came to a new vision of what life could be like as a follower of Jesus. Being heard, being known, and being accepted led to transformation in her life as Jesus challenged her to a new vision of what God's reign would hold. Through authentic relationship and faithful community, persons find deeper meaning in their lives. Making connections and engaging the story contribute to a congregational ministry of making disciples that helps people grow into faithful disciples who walk through life's challenges and opportunities loving God and neighbor. Together we forge a vision of God's reign that draws us forward into new life.

In conclusion, servant leaders are those who follow in Jesus' steps of love, taking on the mind of Christ as they go on God's errands in the word, loving the outcast and oppressed and working for justice. This is the communion of grace in which a congregational ministry of forming faith is undertaken, a communion in which each person plays a valued role, using his or her gifts in a nonhierarchical partnership as go-betweens on behalf of God and the Christian community. In this communion, disputes over who is the greatest have been left behind. As we journey together as God's pilgrim people, each person is valued, and each person has a role in servant leadership in the design for forming faith addressed in the next chapter, "Growing in Communion with God and All of Creation."

Toward Creating a Congregational Ministry of Making Disciples

FOLLOWING IN THE STEPS OF LOVE

Discuss the main ideas of this chapter with your planning team for a congregational ministry of making disciples. What insights have you gained? What questions do you have?

Shared Ministry of Serving—Diakonia

Servant leadership is critically important for following in the steps of love in a congregational ministry of forming faith.

New Testament model of servant ministry:
- ❧ Nonhierarchical partnership of all the people of God
- ❧ Go-betweens on behalf of God and the Christian community

Laity and the ministry of serving:
- ❧ All baptized called to servant ministry—one order of servant ministry
- ❧ Church as servant community—community of the Servant
- ❧ Mind and mission of Christ taken on in daily life

Deacons and the ministry of serving:
- ❧ Has focused expression of serving all the people, particularly the poor and oppressed—another order of servant ministry
- ❧ Performs errand on behalf of God to care for the poor
- ❧ Serves in the intersection of community and the congregation
- ❧ Embodies servant ministry
- ❧ Articulates a vision of the church's participation in Christ's ministry with the poor and oppressed
- ❧ Leads all of the people of God in servant ministry that follows Jesus' steps of love

Elder or priest and the ministry of serving:
- ❧ Has focused expression of spiritual leadership and pastoral oversight—a third order of servant ministry
- ❧ Serves as public representative of the church's servant ministry

ᨀ Leads God's pilgrim people in worship and prayer

ᨀ Leads persons to faith in Jesus Christ

ᨀ Leads study of Scripture and the Christian tradition

ᨀ Exercises pastoral supervision in organizing the congregation for service

ᨀ Leads pilgrim people in obedience to God's mission in the world

Jesus and the ministry of serving:

ᨀ Jesus as the mandate and model for the servant ministry of all of the people of God, lay and ordained

ᨀ Jesus unites Word and service in servant ministry

ᨀ Servant ministry as a spiritual partnership between Jesus Christ and all of the people of God

A Communion of Servant Leaders

Challenge to take the New Testament understanding seriously that all of God's people, lay and ordained, participate in a non-hierarchical partnership of go-betweens on behalf on God and the Christian community.

All of the ministries of the church are of equal importance in a congregational ministry of making disciples.

Every baptized Christian has a vocation of servant ministry, and every person has the capacity for a role in servant leadership.

A servant nature is part of one's being whereas leadership is bestowed or acquired.

Qualities of servant leaders:

ᨀ Caring and accepting

ᨀ Pointing the way—having a goal, shared decision making and skills in problem-solving

ᨀ Listening

ᨀ Tolerance of imperfection

ᨀ Faith in God's love and grace, faith in God's care for creation, faith that God will use the servant leader's life for the transformation of others

Tasks of Servant Ministry:

ᨀ Making connections

~❧ Engaging the story
~❧ Hearing the story
~❧ Drawing out questions of faith
~❧ Entering into honest conversation
~❧ Coming to a shared vision

Other Suggestions for Reflecting and Planning

These suggestions can be used for individual reflection, for discussion in a Christian education event for youth or adults, or for sharing with a team who is designing a congregational ministry of making disciples.

1. Two proposals from the work of Eric Law are helpful in building communion and preparing servant leadership:

Respectful Community Guidelines

R = take RESPONSIBILITY for what you say and feel without blaming others.
E = engage in EMPATHETIC listening.
S = be SENSITIVE to differences in communication styles.
P = PONDER what you hear and feel before you speak.
E = EXAMINE your own assumptions and perceptions.
C = keep CONFIDENTIALITY.
T = TOLERATE ambiguity because we are *not* here to debate who or what is right or wrong.[39]

"Mutual Accountability"

This is a process that invites full participation in a group. The leader/convenor names the topic or question and then invites another person to share. For example, "Tom, would you like to share your thoughts on this question?" Tom can then share his thoughts or say, "Pass," if he chooses. Tom then invites another person to share. This continues until every person in the group has had an opportunity to speak and to invite someone to share. Law's method was designed for and is especially helpful in multicultural groups, but it works in any setting and helps each person in a group find her or his voice.[40]

2. Exercise for identifying and describing faith mentors in our lives: On this chart or on a timeline of your life, note the significant life events that shaped your life. You may or may not have identified these experiences as explicitly religious. For example, you might name a family move during childhood, or a job change. Once you have identified the experience, then make note of the persons who were present with you in some way during this life event. Reflect on how God used that person in your life and make note of the ways they influenced your growth in faith.

SIGNIFICANT LIFE EVENTS	PERSONS WHO WERE THERE	HOW GOD USED THESE PERSONS	HOW THEY INFLUENCED MY LIFE OF FAITH

3. Reflect on the previous exercise then share with others what you observe and how your observations contribute to thinking about servant ministry and servant leadership.

Additional Reading for This Chapter

Mentoring/Making Connections

Daloz, Laurent A. *Mentor: Guiding the Journey of Adult Learners*. San Francisco: Jossey-Bass, 1999.

English, Leona M. *Mentoring in Religious Education*. Birmingham: Religious Education Press, 1998.

Matthaei, Sondra Higgins. *Faith Matters: Faith-Mentoring in the Faith Community*. Valley Forge, Pa.: Trinity Press International, 1996.

Zachary, Lois J. *The Mentor's Guide: Facilitating Effective Learning Relationships.* San Francisco: Jossey-Bass, 2000.

Engaging the Story

Groome, Thomas H. *Christian Religious Education: Sharing Our Story and Vision.* San Francisco: Harper & Row, 1980.

Murray, Dick. *Teaching the Bible to Adults and Youth.* Nashville: Abingdon Press, 1987.

Wimberly, Anne Streaty. *Soul Stories: African American Christian Education.* Revised Edition. Nashville: Abingdon Press, 2006.

Coming to a Shared Vision

Law, Eric H. F. *Sacred Acts, Holy Change: Faithful Diversity and Practical Transformation.* St. Louis: Chalice Press, 2002.

———. *The Wolf Shall Dwell with the Lamb: A Spirituality for Leadership in a Multicultural Community.* St. Louis: Chalice Press, 1993.

CHAPTER FOUR

Growing in Communion
with God and All
of Creation

*For as in one body we have many members, and not all the members have
the same function, so we, who are many, are one body in Christ, and individually we are members one of another. We have gifts that differ according
to the grace given to us: prophecy, in proportion to faith; ministry, in ministering; the teacher, in teaching; the exhorter, in exhortation; the giver, in
generosity; the leader, in diligence; the compassionate, in cheerfulness.*
(Rom 12:4-8)

The New Testament churches must not have been much different
from some of our churches today in their struggle to be the
church. Disputes over leadership (1 Cor 1:10-12) including choosing sides and boasting about the wisdom of the teachings of their
various leaders (1 Cor 1:26-31) caused major conflicts in the church
at Corinth. And yet they still saw themselves as "spiritual." According to commentator Gordon Fee, Paul's letter to the church at
Corinth points out that while "the Corinthians *think* of themselves
as the one—'spiritual' . . . *in fact* they are the other—'divided.' "[1]
Paul tells the Corinthians that you cannot be spiritual *and* divided.
Paul wants the Corinthians "to stop *thinking* like the people of this
present age" and "he wants them to stop *behaving* like the people
of the present age."[2] Rather than focusing on self-promotion or
promotion of others, Paul wants them to think and act like the
body of Christ focusing on God. For Paul, the body of Christ is one
body with all parts of the body seen as essential for doing Christ's
work in the world. The emphasis is on unity with diversity.

63

We would not have to look far in our lives or in our churches to find the things of the present age that separate us from God and our ministry of following in Jesus' steps of love. We find our personal lives derailed from doing God's will by the distractions of modern society such as acquiring status, gaining power, and accumulating wealth and possessions. Our churches are also divided by conflicts over many questions such as who is welcome in our midst and questions about stewardship of resources and leadership.

In order to create a congregational ministry of forming faith that provides authentic relationship, faithful community, and deeper meaning for those who are on a pilgrimage of faith, we need to do our best to leave dissension behind. We need to find ways of remembering that as God's pilgrim people we are called to live in a communion of grace as servant ministers on errands for God in the church and in the world. Taking on this new perspective about our congregational life is so critical because the way we live our lives together is most formative for those who are seeking to grow in faith. In the words of author Roberta Bondi:

> A knowledge of God cannot be taught or learned apart from living out a life that is a reflection of who God is. . . . Knowledge of God does not consist of a set of answers to a list of questions. It is more like the way a wife knows her husband, or a husband knows his wife. The knowledge husband and wife have of each other includes a profound respect for the otherness of the other; based in love, each seeks to preserve the integrity of the other, allowing the other to be without simply becoming an extension of the spouse. It is a knowledge that comes out of living together, responding to each other's daily interests and needs, being shaped by a deep caring for the other. It is a transforming knowledge.[3]

In other words, when we live together in the church as a Christian family, the intentionality of a shared life creates a formative community in which all of the members of the family do their best to live a Christian life in the midst of the many distractions of society. The family becomes a communion of grace in which each person respects and cares about the other. And God's presence in these relationships is the source of transformed lives.

The same is true of the church. Maria Harris argues that "curriculum is an activity, a *practice* of a people" and *each* person is called by God to a Christian way of life and a ministry of serving.[4] In other words, the way God's people live their lives becomes the curriculum that teaches others what it means to be Christian. Everything we do, in word and action, in the church and in our daily lives, teaches others about the Christian life. More formative power comes through our actions than through our words when the members of the church provide models of a faithful life that are essential to the curriculum of forming faith. This is contrasted to our usual understanding that curriculum consists of printed resources that we use in our teaching. Harris proposes a framework for Christian faith formation based first in the way of life of the community of faith, for which she uses the Greek word *koinonia*, "the curriculum of community." Harris then looks at the interrelationship of the nature and tasks of four other curriculum areas of the church's life: prayer (*leitourgia*), teaching (*didache*), proclamation (*kerygma*), and serving (*diakonia*). This model is an effective design because it lifts up these five areas of the church's life and mission as curriculum for forming faith, proposing concrete ideas for how to shape teaching and learning activities in each area.

In the past, this approach to Christian faith formation has been called "socialization" or "enculturation" by educational theorists.[5] In practical terms, it means that persons learn to live a Christian life by being with those who are already practicing a Christian life. We might even call this an apprenticeship model. When we share our pilgrimage of faith in a communion of grace, we have models of faithful living and faith mentors readily accessible to us. We can hear what they say. We can observe what they do. In the example of the formative process in the early Methodist movement, John Wesley wanted parents, teachers, and members of the early Methodist societies to be patterns of the Christian life for those who were seeking to grow in communion with God.[6] In the Methodist meetings, Wesley frequently read letters from persons who shared the story of their faith journeys so that others could hear how they were meeting the challenges of growing in communion with God. These role models were life patterns for new Christians to follow. If we want to create this kind of environment for cultivating faith in our own congregations, we need to leave our divisiveness behind and celebrate the gifts that each member of God's pilgrim people brings to the servant community.

Thinking, Reflecting, Acting

Visit another church and see what you can learn about the identity of that congregation from your visit, for example, mission, values, expectations, hospitality.

Think of times in your congregation when you felt at home or when you did not feel welcome. What was happening that caused you to feel this way?

Unity, Diversity, and Charism

I cannot emphasize enough how important it is for a congregation to be intentional about growing toward this vision of living in a communion of grace as the foundation for a congregational ministry of making disciples. A congregation needs to find its unity in loving God and loving neighbor as the body of Christ while celebrating the diversity of God-given gifts in its midst.

A picture of the rich diversity of gifts in the body of Christ begins to emerge in the passage from Romans 12:4-8. Paul uses the Greek word *charisma* (charism) for gifts: "having charisms which differ in accordance with the grace given to us."[7] In a discussion of Paul's theology, James Dunn wrote that the use of this term (*charisma*) is unique to Paul in the New Testament in his interpretation of *charisma* as a "concrete materialization of God's grace."[8] Applying this idea to our discussion, God's grace is seen and made known through the diversity of gifts in the members of God's pilgrim people, and the use of those gifts is one way that God's grace is experienced by others through servant ministry. We are not to be boastful of what we or others have or do, but we are to serve with humility and celebrate all that God has given each member of the body of Christ by using our gifts through word and deed for the benefit of others—loving God by loving our neighbor. Because our gifts are to be used, Paul ties charism to *praxis*. Dunn noted, "The charism is the contribution which the individual member makes to the whole, its function within the body as a whole."[9] In other words, *praxis* is the active use of one's charism in serving others on behalf of God and the Christian community. These diverse gifts could be shared in a variety of ways in the church and community, such as chairing committees, preparing a meal to be shared with others, building a house for Habitat for Humanity, singing in the choir, or cleaning the church building. We contribute our gifts to the body of Christ to be used on behalf of others. And this brings us to a third word Paul uses with charism, *diakonia*, meaning "diversity of acts of service . . . enabled by divine power."[10] *Charisma, praxis*, and *diakonia* (gifts, action, and service) are given by God to a communion of grace whose members are seeking to live faithful lives in a nonhierarchical partnership of go-betweens on behalf of God and the Christian community.

This charismatic (gifted) community enriched by the many God-given gifts of its individual members functions as the community of Christian formation, and we need to remember that every member has gifts that are of value to the body (Rom 12:4-6) in this task of making disciples. The question may arise whether or not some gifts are appropriate to the mission and ministry of the body of Christ. In response to this issue, Dunn observed that Paul's "extended counsel against speaking in tongues in the assembly makes clear in 1 Cor 14:1-25 that the test of a charism within the charismatic community is its benefit to the community at large."[11] The church at Corinth was in conflict because some of the Corinthians believed that speaking in tongues was the sign of those who were most spiritual, but as Fee noted, "they have a spirituality that has religious trappings (asceticism, knowledge, tongues) but has abandoned rather totally genuinely Christian ethic, with its supremacy of love."[12] Because of Paul's emphasis on the mutual interdependence in the charismatic community, he did not rule out any God-given gifts, but he did understand that all gifts were of equal importance, and every gift should be used to build up the body of Christ in love. In light of our discussion in the previous chapter about the nature of servant ministry as a non-hierarchical partnership, Dunn's summary of Paul's beliefs adds to our reflection:

> No members should regard their charisms as of lesser value or of too little significance or opt out from the body's functioning (1 Cor. 12:15-16). No members should regard the charisms of others as dispensable or unnecessary (1 Cor. 12:21). Common respect and care for one another should rise above all diversity of function, however insignificant, however great (1 Cor. 12:22-26).[13]

Paul's message to the church at Corinth was that all charisms have value, but any charism that divides the church is not put to good use and is, therefore, not appropriate for building up the body of Christ. Gifts are not for the benefit of self but are to be used with humility in loving God and neighbor.

What Paul has offered us is a vision of the church as the embodiment of Christ in the culture in which we live. We make Christ known, through God's grace, in word and deed by serving others. Every member of God's pilgrim people is indispensable and has gifts to be used in servant ministry following in Jesus' steps of love. Our goal in forming faith is to help pilgrims in faith learn the Christian tradition and discover their own gifts in order to find ways to use them in a vocation of loving God and loving neighbor in servant ministry.

Thinking, Reflecting, Acting

On the left-hand side of a sheet of paper, write the names of five people you know in your congregation. Beside each name, write the God-given gifts you have seen in that person. In another column, write the ways that person uses her or his gifts in the church.

> Make a similar list for yourself. What are your God-given gifts and how do you use them in the life of the congregation?

A Ministry of Forming Faith

It may seem at this point that I have taken great pains to propose particular language to identify the theology and goals of a congregational ministry of making disciples: "pilgrimage in faith," "communion of grace," "God's pilgrim people," "charism," and "servant ministry" to name a few. The reason for this is that the language we use to talk about a ministry of forming faith expresses an image and creates a vision for what it is that we are trying to do and why we are doing it. It is this vision that gives us direction for our planning. For example, there are processes of faith formation in every world religion—and each has its own language and vision—so it is important to state that although much of what this book addresses would relate to other religious traditions, it is written in the language, and therefore the theology, of the Christian tradition. A subsequent narrowing of discussion will happen as you use language about Christian faith formation from your own particular denominational tradition to articulate your own vision and goals. So my attempt to be clear about language invites you to think carefully about the language you would use to describe your congregational ministry of making disciples.

A few other concepts for Christian faith formation still need clarification. In previous writing, I have chosen to use the language of "Christian *faith* formation" rather than "Christian *spiritual* formation" to name our task because it points to an intentional process of cultivating faith within a particular religious tradition. I also use it to emphasize more than the spiritual or inner life, a common focus in discussions of spirituality. Christian faith formation means cultivating the inner life of growing in our relationship with God and taking on the mind of Christ, as well as the outer witness to God's love, a vocation of loving our neighbor.

In the past, I argued that the process of Christian faith formation is the heart of our educational ministry: "The ministry of Christian education addresses the tasks of shaping Christian identity and vocation *through* faith formation by helping us develop our relationship with God so that we may witness to our love for God by loving our neighbor."[14] In this definition, Christian faith formation is named as the process that guides a person's growth in faith and contributes to a Christian lifestyle of loving God and neighbor. For me, Christian faith formation not only points to instruction in faith, but it also includes providing opportunities for persons to experience God's love, as well as helping persons learn the skills of study and critical reflection so that they are able to think about matters of faith and interpret the meaning of faith for their own lives. Evidence of this growth of faith is found in their daily lives.

But the process of Christian faith formation is not complete without transformation. Robert A. Evans wrote that "transformation calls for nothing less than a *metanoia* or conversion that encompasses the whole person and society. The conversion affects relationships among God's children—the whole of creation. . . . The coming reign of God means modifications of commitments and patterns of living."[15] In other words, lives are radically changed by God's work of transformation. This description highlights our discussion about being conformed to the mind of Christ, responding to the call to servant ministry through our baptism, and participating in a communion of grace that carries out a ministry of serving others in the world. Within this basic understanding of transformation, there are the transformations that take place in individual lives as persons take on the mind and mission of Christ, the transformation that occurs in a congregation coming to understand itself as a servant community following in Jesus' steps of love, and the transformation that happens in the wider community and world when God's people actively love their neighbor. In a ministry of forming faith, all of these types of transformation come into play. However, it is not enough for individuals to have an experience of being transformed by God's grace without responding to it through changed commitments and pattern of life through servant ministry. It is not enough for us to focus on individuals and not consider the need for transformation in the body of Christ. It is not enough for us to focus on the transformation of individuals and the congregation without considering the transformation that is needed in the wider community as we make ourselves available as vehicles of God's grace in situations of oppression and injustice.

Ultimately, transformation comes from God's grace in Jesus Christ at work in us through the Holy Spirit. Transformation is a gift from God, a concrete manifestation of God's grace. All of our efforts in offering the best Christian faith formation our church can provide will not cause transformation. God invites us into relationship, and it is only when we experience God's love and forgiveness in our hearts that we are truly transformed. The servant communion participates in nurturing this relationship by preparing persons to repent of their sins and receive God's redemptive grace so that they might be transformed for a life focused on love of God and neighbor.[16] And the church also prepares the members of the faith community to support those who are responding to God's love through the prompting of the Holy Spirit. This role certainly includes an element of holding persons accountable for faith and life, but it also includes participating in the mutual interdependence of a communion of grace in which the joys and the burdens of the pilgrimage in faith are shared.

Through formation and transformation, the process of Christian faith formation cultivates growth in Christian identity and Christian vocation. I define Christian identity as coming to know oneself as a Christian, having assimilated the values, beliefs, and lifestyle of one who professes to be a follower of Jesus Christ through study, discernment, and reflection in order to bring life experience into dialogue with the tradition of the church. This understanding points to an assumption that Christian identity is formed through participation in the communion of faith with its long history of faithful servants who are leading the way. It also means that our ministry of forming faith includes instruction and nurture, formation and transformation, reflection and action.

As persons grow in their identity as Christians, they also grow in Christian vocation or discipleship on their faith pilgrimage, using their gifts on behalf of others. So discernment and development of gifts become a critical part of an individual's pilgrimage in faith in order to grow in a vocation of servant ministry. James Fowler wrote that "Vocation is the response a person makes with his or her total self to the address of God and to the calling of partnership."[17] For Fowler, partnership means that we are carrying on God's work in the world. We use our God-given gifts in servant ministry on behalf of God and the Christian community. Frederick Buechner offered another way to think about vocation when he wrote that vocation it is "the place where your deep gladness and the world's deep hunger meet."[18] In other words, as persons claim their inner nature as servant, great joy comes from sharing their gifts in a servant ministry that meets the needs of the world. Discipleship through servant ministry is our vocation of following in Jesus' steps of love, loving God and all of creation. So a pilgrimage in faith is not only about experiencing God's forgiveness and grace but also about responding to God's grace through a vocation of serving.

Growth in Christian identity and vocation continues throughout one's pilgrimage in faith. But this growth is not sequential—first Christian identity and then Christian vocation—because we are called to practice a Christian way of life *while* we are learning our Christian faith tradition and growing in our identity and vocation as followers of Christ in a communion of grace. In other words, our experience of practicing a Christian life through serving others will raise questions about our personal faith and our shared faith tradition, and what we learn about our shared faith tradition will inform and shape our way of serving. Growing in Christian identity and vocation happens in relation to each other, and each is necessary to the other. Our Christian faith formation is not complete if we only learn the tradition of the church without considering how it guides and influences our life of loving God and neighbor. Likewise, if we only try to practice a Christian way of life without ever learning why we do so, our Christian faith formation will not be complete, and it will be difficult for us to continue in this way of life. And in the midst of our living and learning, God is at work in this process so that we might be transformed.

> **Thinking, Reflecting, Acting**
>
> As you think about your own growth in faith, what were the elements of formation (relationships, studies, experiences) that shaped your faith?
>
> When have you experienced transformation in your own life of faith? (There may have been one or more points that seem significant to you.)

Growing in Communion with God— A Vision for Forming Faith

In *Making Disciples*, I used research into John Wesley's theology and the resulting formative practices of the early Methodist movement to propose a model for Christian faith formation based on the belief that God desires to be in relationship with us and provides a way for that relationship to grow. This pilgrimage in faith is a process of growing in relationship to God, a relationship defined by communion. God invites us into communion with the Trinity, and, as we respond to God's invitation to relationship with faith and love, our communion with God deepens through the saving work of Jesus Christ and the enabling work of the Spirit. In other words, this is a two-way relationship that grows with God's acts of grace and our responsive acts of love in heart and life— love of God and love of neighbor, a response that is evident in changed lives. It is a relationship that grows over a lifetime. The vision of the coming reign of God draws us forward to a time when we come to fully love God and neighbor and live together with God and creation in full communion. To become a disciple of Christ means growing in our Christian identity of belonging to God and our Christian vocation of discipleship, following in the steps of love through servant ministry.

Throughout this book, we have considered what it means to live in communion with God and one another. As we move toward creating a ministry of making disciples, I want to lift up the main aspects of this vision of a communion of grace that is the home and curriculum for a congregational ministry of making disciples. First, a communion of grace continues *a long line of God's pilgrim people* ever moving forward to a deeper relationship with God. Those who have gone before are our Christian family and members of our communion of grace. Within this communion, persons continue to grow in their relationship with God in Christ through the work of the Spirit in the curriculum of shared faith and practice. Through participation in the relationships and experiences of the congregation, persons receive God's invitation to an ever-deepening relationship with the triune God. Through the work of the Spirit, persons are conformed to the mind of Christ as they prepare to carry on Christ's servant ministry in the world.

In a communion of grace, we recognize that *God is a participant in all that we do*—in making connections, engaging the story, and coming to a shared vision. God not only is a participant but also gives us the grace to do these things. We could do none of this on our own. It is through God's manifestation of grace in Christ and in the gifts of the pilgrim people that we find mutual authentic relationship, not only with each other but also with God and creation. We are bound together by the interdependence of our shared life in Christ and through the enabling presence of the Holy Spirit that we find deeper meaning for our lives. In a communion of grace, we find a sense of being at home through the interdependence of our shared relationships and faith commitments.

In a communion of grace, *forming faith begins with hospitality*. We are challenged by God's grace to love every human being as our neighbor because he or she is a child of God. We are invited to welcome the diversity around us and the presence of God made known to us in the stranger. We are challenged to stand against oppression and injustice in this world and to embody God's love of all creation. This is the dangerous love of the great commandment because it means that a communion of grace puts loving God and God's creation first over the ways of the world.

A communion of grace is characterized by interdependence as the members of the body of Christ recognize their need for one another and celebrate the God-given gifts each person brings to the life of the church. *A communion of grace is one in the body of Christ but also recognizes the necessity of diversity for knowing God's truth for us and for carrying out Christ's servant ministry in the world.* As a result, servant ministry is a spiritual partnership of all the people of God bound together in a servant community established at our baptism. As such, servant ministers are called by God to discover and use their gifts through servant leadership in a Christian vocation of loving God and neighbor.

Thinking, Reflecting, Acting

Discuss your vision for the coming reign of God and the ways this vision can be embodied, made known now, through the life of your congregation.

What other characteristics of a communion of grace would you name?

Growing in Communion with God— A Plan

We have established that persons grow in faith by participating in a community of the faithful, a community that we are calling the servant communion or a communion of grace. One of our concerns in forming faith is that the process of Christian faith formation needs to be intentional. Christian faith formation happens all the time without intentionality, but it might not have the outcome we envision. An intentional process of forming faith includes exploring the truth of faith from the Christian tradition and reinterpreting that truth for our own lives and for our shared vocation of loving God and neighbor. In other words, growing in communion with God requires attention to both heart and life—

the inner life of loving God and the outer life of loving neighbor. Our goal is to cultivate Christian discipleship built on a living faith, a witnessing and serving faith, as persons grow in communion with God and creation.

What follows is a series of figures modified from my previous work in *Making Disciples* that provide the structure and rationale for a congregational ministry of making disciples. Some tools for creating your own congregational ministry of making disciples can be found in the Appendix.[19]

Figure 1
Growing in Communion with God and Creation
Context and Goal

INVITATION TO COMMUNION	DEEPENING COMMUNION	FULL COMMUNION
The Context:	*The Context:*	*The Context:*
The Communion of Grace	**The Communion of Grace**	**The Communion of Grace**
Life patterned after the communion of the Trinity.	Life patterned after the communion of the Trinity.	Life patterned after the communion of the Trinity.
Practicing life in communion with God and neighbor.	Growing in communion with God and neighbor.	Living in communion with God and neighbor.
Beginning to share gifts in servant ministry and servant leadership.	Sharing gifts more widely through servant ministry and servant leadership.	Sharing life and gifts more fully through servant ministry and servant leadership.
Life together as the curriculum for formation in communion.	Nurturing progressive growth in heart and life in communion.	Agents of the coming reign of God by living as communion of grace.
The Goal: Christian / Christian Identity Vocation	***The Goal:*** Christian - Christian Identity Vocation	***The Goal:*** Christian \ Christian Identity Vocation

Figure 1 begins this proposal for a congregational ministry of form-ing faith and embodies several of the themes and assumptions pro-posed in this book. The goal of growing in communion with God and creation is seen in the headings of the three columns represent-ing three phases of growth in faith. The process follows the original proposal from *Making Disciples* that persons grow in faith through a deepening relationship with God through the work of Jesus Christ and the enabling presence of the Spirit on their pilgrimage in faith.

What is deceptive about this figure is that forming faith is not a linear process made up of three easy steps. Growth in faith is not as predictable as depicted here. We have already described the winding road of the pilgrimage when there are detours and delays. So the intention here is to portray the forward progress toward full communion with God, recognizing that the path is often unpre-dictable and challenging. As you can see from this proposal, growth in faith is a matter of degree and never ends. In addition, the "full communion" phase can only point to the qualities of a life of mature faith since full communion ultimately comes when a person completes his or her earthly pilgrimage.

The context for Christian faith formation is a communion of grace that intentionally seeks to conform its life to the pattern of the Trinity through mutual indwelling and room-giving, growing in interdependence and unity as the body of Christ, while celebrating the necessity of the diversity of gifts in its midst. The second item under communion of grace reflects the degree of growth in com-munion. As new Christians, we practice living in communion with God by learning the spiritual disciplines of loving God and begin-ning to offer our God-given gifts on behalf of others. In other words, we "try on" a Christian lifestyle and practice the ways of faith. As Christians grow closer to God and experience God's trans-formation in their lives, God's grace enables an even deeper shar-ing in exploring the meaning of faith and in participating in servant ministry. Growing in communion means that a person is ever growing toward more fully loving God and all of creation.

The role of the congregation in invitation to communion is to be a place of hospitality, welcoming persons into the life of the communion of grace and then to nurture them in their growth in faith through their participation in the life of the church. Nurturing progressive growth in heart and life means that the communion of grace provides opportunities for new relationships and experiences in faith. When the church grows as God's people in a communion of grace, it becomes an agent of the coming reign of God. This means that when others look at the church from the outside, they are able to see glimpses of a future time when persons leave behind the distractions of the present world to fully embody God's purposes in a life of communion.

Our goal and hope for this process of Christian faith formation is that persons will grow in Christian identity and Christian vocation, so that they will come to know themselves as God's pilgrim people who love God by serving others. In Figure 1, growth in Christian identity is weighted in the beginning phase (signified by /), while more weight is on Christian vocation in the final phase (signified by \ ). Growth in Christian identity and Christian vocation continues throughout a person's pilgrimage in faith and needs to be cultivated throughout the entire process, but the emphasis in faith formation changes in each of these phases.

Figure 2
Growing in Communion with God and Creation
"What to Teach"

INVITATION TO COMMUNION	DEEPENING COMMUNION	FULL COMMUNION
What to Teach?	*What to Teach?*	*What to Teach?*
Gaining Christian Tradition and Practice:	Clarifying Christian Tradition and Practice:	Extending Christian Tradition and Practice:
Emphasizes an **instructional** mode of using the resources of the Christian faith—Scripture and tradition—to teach what it means to live as the body of Christ in a communion	Emphasizes a **dialogical** mode of using the resources of the Christian faith—Scripture and tradition—to converse about the meaning of living as the body of Christ in a	Emphasizes an **embodied** mode of using the resources of the Christian faith—Scripture and tradition—to practice life as the body of Christ in a communion of grace by more

of grace by practicing love of God and neighbor.	communion of grace by growing in love of God and neighbor.	fully loving God and neighbor.
Formative Process: Instructing persons in the beliefs and practices of the Christian life.	**Formative Process:** Exploring the beliefs and practices of the Christian life.	**Formative Process:** Embodying the beliefs and practices of the Christian life.
Nurturing the Christian life through spiritual practices. **The Goal:** Christian / Christian Tradition Practice	Nurturing the Christian life through spiritual practices. **The Goal:** Christian - Christian Tradition Practice	Nurturing the Christian life through spiritual practices. **The Goal:** Christian \ Christian Tradition Practice

Figure 2 addresses a basic question for a congregational ministry of forming faith: What to teach. The actual content of the teaching is based on the tradition of the church and your own particular denominational tradition. What is suggested here is that the teaching begins with an emphasis on the instructional mode for new pilgrims who need to know more about the beliefs and shared faith commitment of the communion of grace in order to gain knowledge and understanding of the Christian tradition. The second phase emphasizes a dialogical mode in which honest conversation explores Christian tradition and practice of the Christian life. And the final phase emphasizes an embodied mode in which the lives of pilgrims in faith clearly reflect what it means to live together in communion with God and creation—extending Christian tradition and practice into their lives in the world. You may have noticed that Christian Identity and Christian Vocation have been replaced by Christian Tradition and Christian Practice as the goal in this figure. This is not a change in goal since the terms are related. It is in learning the stories of our family of faith (Christian tradition) that our Christian identity is shaped when we come to know who we are as members of God's family, and Christian practice is another way of talking about discipleship or Christian vocation, our servant ministry in the world.

Each of the three modes of teaching—instructional, dialogical, and embodied—is needed in every phase of growing in communion. What I am suggesting here is that each phase requires a particular emphasis in the mode of formation. For example, dialogue about questions of faith and embodying the Christian life are very important for new Christians, but the emphasis is on helping them learn the Christian tradition as they begin to practice a Christian way of life. So while the emphasis with new Christians is on the instructional mode, the dialogical and embodied modes are also needed for their growth in faith. New Christians need to have opportunities for honest discussion to explore what they are learning more deeply, and they need guidance for practicing a Christian way of life, particularly through opportunities for serving.

Participation in the dialogical and embodied modes grows stronger as persons become more knowledgeable of the Christian tradition and practice of a Christian way of life. While Christian practice is emphasized with more mature Christians, they also need to continue to grow in their knowledge of the Christian tradition.

What should be emphasized here is that there are adults in all of these phases at any one time in the life of the communion of grace, so it is important to provide teaching and learning experiences that move persons who are in different places on their faith pilgrimage toward ever-deepening engagement in the Christian tradition and practices of the Christian life. However, you do not need some kind of assessment tool to determine where each person is in his or her spiritual pilgrimage in order to create a congregational ministry of forming faith. From my own life experience, I know that the Spirit drew me into situations that could teach me something I needed to learn. So by planning a variety of experiences that relate to each of these phases, the needs of the various learners will be addressed as they choose to participate in these teaching and learning events. And their growth will be enhanced by being with others who are in a different place on the pilgrimage of faith. So we can trust that the "self-selection" process guided by the Holy Spirit will provide opportunities that enrich each individual's pilgrimage in faith.

Instructing, exploring, and extending are the key elements of the formative process for growing as a Christian. The pairing of these elements with nurture of the Christian life through spiritual practices contributes to formation of heart and life. By participating in these formative practices, pilgrims open themselves to God's grace and transformation by the Holy Spirit as they prepare to carry on Christ's ministry in the world.

Figure 3
Growing in Communion with God and Creation
"Who Shall Teach?"

INVITATION TO COMMUNION	DEEPENING COMMUNION	FULL COMMUNION
Who Shall Teach?	*Who Shall Teach?*	*Who Shall Teach?*
Qualities:	**Qualities:**	**Qualities:**
1. True dedication to God and to nurturing others on the pilgrimage of faith.	1. True dedication to God and to nurturing others on the pilgrimage of faith.	1. True dedication to God and to nurturing others on the pilgrimage of faith.
2. Knowledge of the Christian tradition and denominational beliefs, as well as Christian practice.	2. Knowledge of the Christian tradition and denominational beliefs, as well as Christian practice.	2. Knowledge of the Christian tradition and denominational beliefs, as well as Christian practice.
3. Commitment to the Christian discipline of nurturing one's own inner and outer lives of faith through practicing the spiritual disciplines, studying the Christian tradition, and serving others.	**3. Commitment to the Christian discipline of nurturing one's own inner and outer lives of faith through practicing the spiritual disciplines, studying the Christian tradition, and serving others.**	3. Commitment to the Christian discipline of nurturing one's own inner and outer lives of faith through practicing the spiritual disciplines, studying the Christian tradition, and serving others.

4. Ability to work with a diverse group of people, recognizing the necessity of diversity for discovering God's truth for our lives of faith.	**4. Ability to work with a diverse group of people, recognizing the necessity of diversity for discovering God's truth for our lives of faith.**	4. Ability to work with a diverse group of people, recognizing the necessity of diversity for discovering God's truth for our lives of faith.
5. Life pattern of servant ministry, embodying the life of Christ by loving God and all of God's creation.	5. Life pattern of servant ministry, embodying the life of Christ by loving God and all of God's creation.	**5. Life pattern of servant ministry, embodying the life of Christ by loving God and all of God's creation.**
6. Evidence of continued growth in communion with God and neighbor through servant leadership.	6. Evidence of continued growth in communion with God and neighbor through servant leadership.	**6. Evidence of continued growth in communion with God and neighbor through servant leadership.**
Servant Teaching Relationships: Instructional relationship	**Servant Teaching Relationships:** Dialogical relationship	**Servant Teaching Relationships:** Mutually accountable relationships
Life pattern	Life pattern	Life pattern
Parent-Child	Teacher-Student	Mutual participation in teaching and learning
The Context: Christian family	**The Context:** Christian family	**The Context:** Christian family

Who shall teach is a second important question for a congregational ministry of forming faith. Servant teaching, as part of a congregational ministry of forming faith, means sharing one's knowledge or experience on the behalf of others' growth in faith and engaging others in exploring the meaning of their own knowledge and experience. We have already established that each person has gifts to contribute to a shared servant ministry in a communion of grace. Sharing gifts is a resource for teaching and learning. This means that if, as we have claimed, the life of the congregation is the curriculum of faith formation, then any encounter or event is a teaching and learning activity. In other words, teaching and learning take place in the context of the shared life of the Christian family, God's pilgrim people, in a communion of grace.

Figure 3 addresses the specific gifts needed for the various forms of servant teaching involved in forming faith. These characteristics apply to designated leaders of classes or governance structures, participants in church events, and even more informal relationships. There are six basic qualities listed, and they are the same for each phase of growing in communion. However, there are two that are highlighted for emphasis in each phase.

An instructional relationship is emphasized when persons first respond to God's invitation to communion. Those who serve as teachers in this phase need to be persons who have a deep commitment to God and to nurturing others on their pilgrimage. They are also persons of memory. They remember what it was like to be new to the faith. They remember times when they stumbled in their faith pilgrimage. They remember how they came to know the Christian tradition. They are open about their own questions of faith. Sometimes these persons are called "companions on the way," "guides," or "mentors," and all have experienced the winding path of a pilgrimage in faith. In addition, these servant teachers need to have good basic knowledge of the Christian tradition and your particular denominational tradition. Much like parents who want the best for their children, these servant teachers do not need to have all the answers, but they do need to be willing to seek out resources and to enter into honest conversation about faith questions. We might describe them as naturally inquisitive, eager to learn, hospitable, and good listeners. In other words, these servant teachers are good life patterns of what it means to walk in faith as followers of Christ.

In the second phase, the same qualities of commitment and knowledge of the Christian and denominational traditions are important, but now the emphasis is on the servant teacher as a life pattern of nurturing one's own inner and outer lives of faith through the practice of spiritual disciplines, studying the Christian tradition, and serving others. Not only are servant teachers a model for these practices, they invite others who are growing in faith to join with them in a deeper exploration of what it means to be Christian and follow in Jesus' steps of love. In this phase, a dialogical relationship is emphasized as teachers and learners together enter into a time of studying, reflecting, questioning, and serving—growing together as servant ministers who are sent by God to carry on God's work in the world. The teacher-student relationship here is, in the best sense of the term, a mentoring relationship in which the servant teachers share wisdom and experience with pilgrims in faith. And this is not a one-way teaching relationship as the servant teacher is also listening and learning from the engagement in study and honest conversation with others. This means that those who teach in this phase of deepening communion with God and creation have an ability to work with a diverse group of people, recognizing the necessity of diversity for discovering God's truth for their shared lives of faith.

In the final phase of full communion with God, the servant teachers also have the qualities we have already discussed, but the emphasis is on the final two qualities in the list. The servant leader provides a clear life pattern of servant ministry in that others are able to observe what it means to embody the life of Christ through love of God and creation in the life of this servant teacher. A second quality is that even though this servant leader seems to be close to God, he or she also demonstrates openness to continued growth in communion with God and creation. While these servant teachers are walking in the steps of love every day, they still open themselves for the work of God's Spirit within, as they continue to grow in knowledge of the Christian tradition and practice of the Christian life. They are life patterns of what it means to be at home in God and participate in the mutually accountable relationships of full communion. This phase is also characterized by participation in mutual teaching and learning as persons engage the questions of faith at an ever deeper level and express their love of God and neighbor in significant ways through servant ministry.

Figure 4
Growing in Communion with God and Creation
"How to Teach": Relationships, Structures, and Practices for
Forming Faith

INVITATION TO COMMUNION	DEEPENING COMMUNION	FULL COMMUNION
How to Teach?	**How to Teach?**	**How to Teach?**
Relationships:	*Relationships:*	*Relationships:*
Individual counsel	Individual counsel	Individual counsel
Instructional mentoring	Dialogical mentoring	Mutual mentoring
Honest conversation	Honest conversation	Honest conversation
Reflection on practice	Reflection on practice	Reflection on practice
Cultivating the Inner Life of Faith	**Cultivating the Inner Life of Faith**	**Cultivating the Inner Life of Faith**
Structures:	*Structures:*	*Structures:*
Worship	Worship	Worship
Lord's Supper	Lord's Supper	Lord's Supper
Spiritual retreat	Spiritual retreat	Spiritual retreat
Spiritual direction	Spiritual direction	Spiritual direction
Covenant groups	Covenant groups	Covenant groups
Practices:	*Practices:*	*Practices:*
Prayer—private and public	Prayer—private and public	Prayer—private and public
Reading and studying Scripture	Reading and studying Scripture	Reading and studying Scripture
Singing the faith	Singing the faith	Singing the faith
Spiritual disciplines such as meditation, silence, fasting	Spiritual disciplines such as meditation, silence, fasting	Spiritual disciplines such as meditation, silence, fasting
Cultivating the Outer Life of Faith	**Cultivating the Outer Life of Faith**	**Cultivating the Outer Life of Faith**

Structures:	**Structures:**	**Structures:**
Gift discernment	Gift discernment	Gift discernment
Bible study	Bible study	Bible study
Research into the Christian tradition	Research into the Christian tradition	Research into the Christian tradition
Small groups for making connections, engaging the story, sharing a vision	Small groups for making connections, engaging the story, sharing a vision	Small groups for making connections, engaging the story, sharing a vision
Practices:	**Practices:**	**Practices:**
Practicing a Christian life	Practicing a Christian life	Practicing a Christian life
Mission trips	Mission trips	Mission trips:
Participating in outreach ministries	Participating in outreach ministries	Participating in outreach ministries
The Goal: Christian / Christian Tradition Practice	**The Goal:** Christian - Christian Tradition Practice	**The Goal:** Christian \ Christian Tradition Practice

Figure 4 begins to put shape to a design for a congregational ministry of making disciples. Some beginning ideas are proposed here for cultivating the inner and outer lives of faith. Three categories are offered: relationships, structures, and practices. I would argue that relationships are the most influential element in forming faith. For persons who are growing into a deeper relationship with God, having guides and companions on their pilgrimage is critical. We know that community is needed for faith formation, so relationships within the servant communion make a significant contribution to the curriculum of making disciples. Just as the relationship with God deepens on a faith pilgrimage, so do the relationships a pilgrim makes along the way. Individual counsel, formal or informal, is important in each phase of growth. This counsel could come through an appointment with a pastor or counselor, through conversation with a spiritual director, or it could come through informal conversation at a church picnic.

Mentoring by others who have been on the pilgrimage of faith is also important in each phase of the pilgrimage. Because the emphasis for new Christians is on learning the Christian tradition while practicing a Christian life, I have called the mentoring here "instructional mentoring." This corresponds with the first two qualities of teachers in Figure 3. The same parallel follows as persons grow in deepening communion with God. Here dialogical mentoring is emphasized and corresponds with the third and fourth qualities in Figure 3. For those who are further along in their pilgrimage, mutual mentoring emphasizes the last two qualities for servant teachers in Figure 3. Throughout one's pilgrimage, honest conversation about questions and experiences in faith along with reflection on practicing the Christian life through servant ministry is the content of these relationships.

The rest of Figure 4 offers some examples of structures and practices that cultivate the inner and outer lives of faith. I have followed Maria Harris's proposal that study and service build the outer life of faith, whereas spiritual practices nourish our inner life of faith. Some structures such as worship and the Lord's Supper, as well as the practice of prayer, would clearly cultivate the outer life of faith as well. As you make your own design, I encourage you to think creatively about the elements of Christian faith formation already present in your congregational life. You could begin by incorporating all of the relationships, structures, and practices that already exist in your congregation into the format suggested here and then begin to brainstorm possibilities for new forms of relationships, structures, and practices for your congregational ministry of forming faith—always keeping in mind the vision for your ministry.

These proposals point toward the goal of forming faith in a communion of grace, Christian discipleship built on a living faith—a witnessing and serving faith. Formation for growing in communion with God is grounded in faith, finding a new identity in communion, and growing in discipleship—loving God and neighbor through servant ministry. It is my hope that this chapter has given you a framework and some specific ideas about building a communion of grace and creating a congregational ministry of making disciples with God's help. As you go forward, my vision for your church is one of living in communion with the Trinity, following in Jesus' steps of love, and fully loving God and neighbor.

Toward Creating a Congregational Ministry of Making Disciples

GROWING IN COMMUNION WITH GOD AND ALL CREATION

Discuss the main ideas of this chapter with your planning team for a congregational ministry of making disciples. What insights have you gained? What questions do you have?

Unity, Diversity, and Charism

It's time to leave our competitive nature and dissension behind to build a communion of grace where every member of the body of Christ is seen as having value and purpose.

The communion of grace is at the heart of a congregational ministry of making disciples.

The members of the communion of grace make Christ known, through God's grace, in word and deed by serving others.

Every member of God's pilgrim people is indispensable and has gifts to be used in servant ministry following in Jesus' steps of love.

Our goal in forming faith is to help pilgrims in faith discover their own gifts and find ways to use them in a vocation of loving God and neighbor in servant ministry.

A Ministry of Forming Faith

Christian faith formation is a process over a lifetime.

Christian faith formation means cultivating the inner life of growing in our relationship with God and taking on the mind of Christ, as well as the outer witness to God's love, a vocation of loving our neighbor.

Christian faith formation helps persons claim their Christian identity: coming to know oneself as a Christian, having assimilated the values, beliefs, and lifestyle of one who professes to be a follower of Jesus Christ through study, discernment, and reflection in order to bring life experience into dialogue with the tradition of the church.

Christian faith formation helps persons discern and prepare for their Christian vocation: carrying on God's work in the world through servant ministry.

Transformation is God's gift and changes a person's relationship with God and God's creation. The evidence of this transformation is seen in a person's daily life through words and actions.

The servant communion prepares persons for servant ministry through worship, study, and service.

Growing in Communion with God

A communion of grace is the home and curriculum for a congregational ministry of making disciples.

- ❧ *God is a participant in all that we do.*
- ❧ *A communion of grace is part of a long line of God's pilgrim people ever moving forward to a deeper relationship with God.*
- ❧ *Forming faith begins with hospitality.*
- ❧ *A communion of grace is one in the body of Christ but also recognizes the necessity of diversity for knowing God's truth for us and for carrying out Christ's servant ministry in the world.*

An intentional process of faith formation includes exploring the truth of faith with the new generations, as well as claiming that truth in new ways for our own lives and for our shared vocation of loving God and neighbor.

Other Suggestions for Reflecting and Planning

These suggestions can be used for individual reflection, for discussion in a Christian education event for youth or adults, or for sharing with a team who is designing a congregational ministry of making disciples.

1. Gather up all the results of "Other Suggestions for Reflecting and Planning" from each chapter of this book. Have members of

your design team compile the responses to share with the group as a whole.

2. Discuss Figure 1 and develop your own statement of the faith community as the heart of a congregational ministry of forming faith.

3. Discuss Figure 2 and list all of the classes, events, and activities of your congregation.

4. Discuss Figure 3 and name qualities that you might add to the list.

5. Add your own ideas to Figure 4 about structures for cultivating the inner and outer lives of faith.

6. While we have been focusing on pilgrimage of faith along the whole range of adulthood in this book, these figures could also be used to think about the relationships, structures, and practices that nourish children and youth in their pilgrimages in faith. Similar relationships, structures, and practices would need to be translated into age-appropriate form. If the argument here is that life in the communion of grace is the curriculum for forming faith, it would include persons of all ages and abilities. One model for breaking away from age-based Christian education to a community form of Christian education is Charles Foster's "event-based" education.[20] This model fits with our assumption that the shared life of the church is the curriculum for faith formation, and it is built around intergenerational events celebrating important events in the Christian tradition and in persons' lives.

Additional Reading for This Chapter

Foster, Charles R. *Educating Congregations: The Future of Christian Education.* Nashville: Abingdon Press, 1994.

Harris, Maria. *Fashion Me a People: Curriculum in the Church.* Louisville: Westminster/John Knox, 1989.

Moore, Mary Elizabeth Mullino. *Teaching as a Sacramental Act.* Cleveland: Pilgrim Press, 2004.

Vogel, Linda J. *Teaching and Learning in Communities of Faith: Empowering Adults Through Religious Education.* San Francisco: Jossey-Bass, 1991.

CHAPTER FIVE

The Challenges That Lie Ahead

If I speak in the tongues of mortals and of angels, but do not have love, I am a noisy gong or a clanging cymbal. And if I have prophetic powers, and understand all mysteries and all knowledge, and if I have all faith, so as to remove mountains, but do not have love, I am nothing. If I give away all my possessions, and if I hand over my body so that I may boast, but do not have love, I gain nothing. (1 Cor 13:1-3)

Love never ends. But as for prophecies, they will come to an end; as for tongues, they will cease; as for knowledge, it will come to an end. For we know only in part, and we prophesy only in part; but when the complete comes, the partial will come to an end. When I was a child, I spoke like a child, I thought like a child, I reasoned like a child; when I became an adult, I put an end to childish ways. For now we see in a mirror, dimly, but then we will see face to face. Now I know only in part; then I will know fully, even as I have been fully known. And now faith, hope, and love abide, these three; and the greatest of these is love. (1 Cor 13:8-13)

I love the church—most of the time. It has been a significant part of my life in the past and continues to nourish my pilgrimage in faith. Growing up in a pastor's family in another century meant that our lives centered on the rhythms of the church's life. Youth groups, sunrise services, Sunday school classes, campfires at church camp, choir, candlelight midnight Christmas Eve services, singing hymns at sunset out on the lawn at the Sunday evening service, mission trips, and potluck dinners still remain as vivid images in my mind. And each of those images is accompanied by the persons who were there, those who were life patterns of faithful living, those who answered my questions, those who asked tough questions, and those who stood by me in times of struggle and doubt. These formative relationships and events shaped my life and led me to teach others what it means to be servant leaders in the church.

I also don't like the church—some of the time. It is a human institution plagued with all of the things that serve to separate us from God and from doing God's work in the world. New Christians are often shocked when they discover the inner workings of the institutional church. They sometimes find pettiness, territoriality, and dissension at the heart of the church. As anyone knows who has attended a regional or national or global church meeting, there are power plays and the posturing of politics. As anyone knows who has been involved in ministry committees or has tried to find their way into ordained ministry in their denomination, there are politics and hierarchies that block women and persons from various racial/ethnic groups from reaching the "top" levels of ministry, if they are accepted into ministry at all. As anyone knows who has associated with local church pastors, there are some who seem to be more focused on their own career opportunities than the mind and mission of Christ. As anyone who has participated in a local church knows, there are conflicts over leadership, over use of the church building, over stewardship, and over ministries. When I see these things, I sometimes wonder if the church can even be the church anymore.

I have a vision of the church as the body of Christ living as a communion of grace, a sign of the reign of God already present in this life. But it is only with manifest trust in God's grace working in the church through the Holy Spirit that I have dared to propose the hopeful vision in this book, a vision of a communion of grace. In this communion, the church, with God's help, tries to live as the body of Christ in the interdependence of mutual indwelling and in the acceptance of diversity through room-giving. God's Spirit draws the church toward becoming a servant communion that recognizes that each person has gifts and graces to share in various forms of servant ministry. This ministry is a nonhierarchical partnership of all Christians who have particular roles in servant ministry and servant leadership as go-betweens on behalf of

God and the Christian community. To live in this communion of grace requires that we affirm every part of the body as critically and equally important for loving God and God's creation, including our neighbors.

It is in this communion of grace that a congregational ministry of forming faith is born and nurtured. God gives us one another and invites us into an ever-deepening relationship, so that together we grow into a communion of grace on our pilgrimage in faith. This is not easy and we cannot create a communion of grace alone. Everything will not be all peace and light on this pilgrimage. We are human beings and the church is a human institution, so there will be sin and grace, ambiguity and compromise, conflict and reconciliation. The difference between any other church and a communion of grace is in how these issues are addressed. To keep our eye on God and accept God's invitation to communion means that we remember that the person before us is always the face of Christ in our midst. As a result, we take time to make connections, engage the story, and come to a shared vision when differences, tension, or conflict arise. In a communion of grace, all differences will not be resolved; all conflict will not be reconciled. But we will agree to make room for the differences while maintaining our shared commitment to Jesus Christ and following in Jesus' steps of love. This is one challenge that lies ahead. *We need to learn to focus on our shared commitment to Christ while we celebrate the diversity among us.* We are called to journey together in faith, hope, and love.

Love Is Eternal

One of the most beautiful chapters in the Bible is 1 Corinthians 13 in which Paul tries to create an image of the Christian way of life for the church at Corinth. As we have discovered, Paul is trying to convince the Corinthians to live together as the body of Christ, using their gifts for building up the church rather than valuing some gifts more highly than others and tearing each other down. According to Gordon Fee, the chapter begins with one of Paul's central arguments: "Paul insisted that *charismata* and good works do not benefit the speaker or doer if he or she does not also have Christian love."[1] Paul continues to build on his argument that love has primacy over all other gifts because love never ends (vv. 8-13). For Paul, gifts will come to an end (v. 8) because they are only partial (v. 9), so gifts, with the exception of love, belong "only to the present."[2] Fee summarized Paul's argument saying, "At the coming of Christ the final purpose of God's saving work in Christ will have been reached; at that point those gifts now necessary for the building up of the church in the present age will disappear, because 'the complete' will have come."[3] What we can draw from this scripture for our discussion is that God has given gifts to each person to be used for building up the ministry and mission of the communion of grace. But if we do not share our gifts in love, they are nothing. *We are not to share our God-given gifts for our own gain but for the benefit of others in love.* This is our second challenge: to humbly use our gifts in love.

Another challenge for the church is that *our vision and knowledge of God is only partial* (v. 9). As Fee wrote, "Our present 'vision' of God, as great as it is, is as nothing when compared to the real thing that is yet to be; it is like the difference between seeing a reflected image in a mirror and seeing a person face to face."[4] Because our vision of God is only partial, we need the whole communion of grace to craft a vision of what lies ahead. Through study of Scripture, prayer, and honest conversation, we share visions of God's purposes in the world from many different perspectives in order to create our vision for a congregational ministry of forming faith. And because we are human, our visions and actions will sometimes be misdirected or flawed and questions will remain. It may be that living with the questions and not rushing to find answers requires the most faith. As Maria Rainer Rilke wrote,

> Be patient toward all that is unsolved in your heart and try to love the *questions themselves*. . . . Do not now seek the answers, which cannot be given to you because you would not be able to live them. And the point is, to live everything. *Live* the ques-

tions now. Perhaps you will then gradually, without noticing it, live along some distant day into the answer."[5]

Remembering that the questions themselves are God's gift to us will help us be patient with ourselves and others. In wrestling with the questions, we will find God's love as well as the courage to move forward in our pilgrimage in faith.

Scripture gives us guidance for our pilgrimage: "faith, hope, and love abide, these three; and the greatest of these is love." (v. 13) Fee believed that this triad appeared in Paul's writing because it was a phrase that was familiar to the early Christians. "Together these words embrace the whole of Christian existence, as believers live out the life of the Spirit in the present age, awaiting the consummation."

- "They have 'faith' toward God, that is, they trust [God] to forgive and accept them through Christ."
- "They also have 'hope' for the future, which has been guaranteed for them through Christ. . . . They are on their way 'home,' destined for an existence in the presence of God that is 'face to face.'"
- "And they have 'love' for one another as they live this life of faith and hope in the context of a community of brothers and sisters of similar faith and hope."[6]

These are gifts to God's people—faith, hope, and love—gifts that sustain their pilgrimage in faith in the present. These are the gifts that build up a communion of grace, the body of Christ carrying on God's work in the world. But in the end, love is eternal and "'continues on into the final glory'" while the work of faith and hope is completed in the present life.[7]

From this passage in 1 Corinthians it is clear that the vision I have shared with you, or any vision that you create for your congregational ministry, is only partial. We have a glimpse of the coming reign of God through the salvation history revealed in Scripture, through the witness of faithful disciples throughout the history of the church, and through our own experiences in faith. It is on these resources that we draw to create our vision and our goals for a congregational ministry of forming faith. In faith we could say that God's communion is already present and glimpses of this communion are made known to us through the Christian tradition and our own experience. And our hope is that God's communion will be made known to others through our efforts to build up the body of Christ using our gifts in a nonhierarchical partnership of servant ministry on behalf of God and the Christian communion.

Moving Forward in Love

We know who we are—God's pilgrim people growing in communion with God—and we know what we need to do to prepare for servant ministry—cultivate our inner and outer lives of faith. We know that we are part of a servant communion, with each one called to use his or her gifts in servant ministry. And we know we are called to be servant leaders, those who have the heart of a servant and are willing to use their gifts with love in building up the body of Christ to carry on Christ's mission in the world.

As we move forward in love, we will have decisions to make, decisions about relationships, structures, and practices in our plan for a congregational ministry of forming faith; decisions about the use of gifts in servant ministry and servant leadership; and decisions about ministry and mission. We have offered two sources that provide different perspectives on the criterion of love to guide decision making. The first comes from 1 Corinthians. Because love is eternal, love, then, becomes the ultimate criterion for all that we do in our congregational ministry of forming faith. The second comes from the great commandment to love God and neighbor. Both of these passages from Scripture teach us that love is our guide and rule. So when questions arise about what to do and how to do it in our ministry of making disciples, we need to ask ourselves, "Does this plan demonstrate love of God and love of neighbor?" "How can we use our God-given gifts with love?" If our plans are not created in love and will result in harm to others, then they have no place in a communion of grace intent on forming faith.

A plan for a congregational ministry of making disciples cannot be designed and accomplished in a day or a week or a year. This is a ministry that will grow over time with God's grace. You need to start where people are and develop the following elements of the plan:

Create a Vision

Explore visions. Begin conversations throughout your congregation by studying Scripture, exploring the history of the church and your own local congregation, and sharing personal faith experience to create a vision for a congregational ministry of making disciples. What is God calling you to do? Where is the need in the world? What do you want to accomplish? Take time to listen to one another and come to a shared sense of your vision. Once you have it, express your vision through a mission statement for your church, print it on your Sunday bulletins or in your weekly newsletter, and find other ways to always hold that vision before your congregation as you shape your mission and ministry.

Rehearse the vision. Live out your vision in worship, in committee meetings, in one-on-one relationships, in your homes, on the street, and at your places of work. Tell God's Story, create rituals and symbols, sing your vision, and share it with others. Practice living as if the reign of God is here now by loving God and neighbor as best you can every day.

Review and renew your vision. At least once a year, review and renew your vision. The study and experience of the communion of grace will bring new insight to the understanding of your vision. New members will bring new ideas and visions to contribute. World events will challenge your vision and call for reflecting once again about how God is calling you forward. New experiences in ministry and mission will provide clarification of your vision. Use different language and images to find a variety of ways to express your vision throughout the life of the church and community. Create a liturgy or ritual such as a watchnight covenant service for renewing your vision.

Build Communion

Build relationships—make connections, engage the story. In your congregational ministry of forming faith, provide a variety of ways and places for persons of different ages and backgrounds to meet each other. You already will have some of these such as coffee time before or after church, Sunday school classes, work groups, Bible study, and prayer groups. But be creative about this. I've known pastors who met young adults for coffee at the local bookstore and women who got to know each other when quilting. At one church, the pastors met with medical personnel going off duty at the hospital at midnight to discuss questions of faith that arose in their medical practice. Others have formed deep friendships on mission trips. In any of these places where persons meet, encourage them to follow the process of making connections, engaging the story through honest sharing about faith, and sharing a vision of God's direction for their lives and the life of the communion of grace. God is in the in-between of these relationships, and the Holy Spirit will guide persons into relationships that have meaning for them.

Discern and develop gifts. Some gifts just emerge as persons share in the life of a communion of grace, but there are others that will need to be discovered and cultivated in those who think they have nothing to offer. Some churches use one of the gift-discernment studies that are available in print. But gifts are also discovered through the invitation to share ministry tasks in the church, such as preparing a meal, helping with a children's choir, planting flowers, leading a group, teaching a class, painting and decorating rooms, reading Scripture in worship, joining a work project in the community, and preparing church mailings. Watch what people are doing, especially those who are doing things for others. Ask people to name someone who would have skills for a particular ministry. It's easy for churches to fall into the pattern of having the same people involved in most of the tasks of the church. Look for the quiet ones. The key is to invite different persons to participate in the study and practice of the Christian way of life, to share in servant ministry.

Practice the Christian life—live the vision. Our role in a con-gregational ministry of forming faith is to live the vision, "to help the church become God's hands and feet, heart and mind—Christ's body in the world in which we live. When per-sons live in the intersections of life *as if* the reign of God is now, they become vehicles of God's grace [for others]."[8] We have learned that practicing a Christian way of life means growing in communion with God and our neighbor and sharing in a non-hierarchical partnership of servant ministry in the world. The formative task here is to invite persons to practice the Christian life by participating in servant ministry using their gifts. This means giving persons an opportunity to serve wherever they are. For example, my mother is 89 years old and lives in a care center. She wanted to do more with her life than work cross-word puzzles and watch TV, so she makes leper bandages to send to India each year with a mission team from Tennessee. Persons do not have to be young or able-bodied to find a way to serve others. So be creative and find connections between gifts and the needs in the world.

Organize for Cultivating the Inner and Outer Lives of Faith

The last chapter began to offer some ideas for nurturing per-sons' inner and outer lives of faith. One thing I have not men-tioned is all the resources that are available that help you grow closer to God through the practice of spiritual disciplines. I have added some books at the end of this chapter, but there may also be retreat centers, spiritual directors from other denominations, stud-ies on how to pray, meditation tapes, and many other resources for those who want to use devotional practices to open themselves to God. The same would be true for learning the Christian tradition. If you live near a church college or seminary, invite teachers to do workshops or classes for your congregation. Look for ways to serve in your community and beyond. Many needs are often invisible to us. Ask social service agencies or other churches about service opportunities. Look for volunteer positions that members of the servant communion could do. Help with tutoring children, teaching English language skills, visiting the sick, or teaching new mothers how to care for babies. There is a whole world outside the walls of the church, and everyone who serves will find that without expecting it, their faith will be enriched through service.

Assess the Need

One of the most important steps in servant ministry is assessing the need. This does not mean just looking at the need through our own eyes, but through the eyes of others as well. A group that is interested in a particular justice issue, for example, could research the issue to learn about the issues and people involved. They could visit those who are affected by that issue to listen to their stories and hear how they think the church could help and then work together to create a plan for addressing the issue.

Act

Once all the study and discussing and planning is done, it is time to act, although sometimes as Christians we may need to act first and discuss later, especially in situations where persons are being hurt or threatened. Here's an example. After 9/11, the threat to those who were "different" was high. In Kansas City, a businessman who originally came from India was murdered. Other United States citizens were assaulted. During this time, the telephone at the Islamic Center was answered with patience and grace. Many of the calls brought words of hate and threats of death, but other calls came from women who offered to accompany the Muslim women to the grocery store or to their children's doctor appointments. Students on our campus did the same for our Korean students who had received threats when they went off campus to their churches or to the grocery store. Their children were being threatened in school as well. Sometimes servant ministers need courage to act against life-destroying practices in order to love all of God's creation.

Following in Jesus' steps of love means that we are called to stand against the tides of hate spreading across our land. And now with the war in Iraq and the border wars, the hate has spread to anyone who looks different—to immigrants, whether legal or illegal. It is easy to forget that each person we meet is the face of Christ. God calls us to love all of our neighbors as children of God. In our time, it is helpful to remember that many who came to this country, including our own ancestors, found freedom to worship God and love neighbor, teaching others through their Christian way of life. So we need to explore what it means to be hospitable in the communion of grace. How will we love all of God's creation in our daily lives?

The Bread of Christ

Forming faith in a communion of grace calls us to a new way of being in the world. We are called to be servants first, offering our God-given gifts in love on behalf of others. I believe that the greatest challenge that lies ahead is the *call to us to become the bread of Christ for others*. In James Dunn's discussion of Paul's theology, he wrote that in Paul's emphasis on the body of Christ, "Paul saw a close connection between the broken bread (= Christ's body) and the church as one body . . . *one* bread, therefore *one* body."[9] During Holy Communion, eating the bread and drinking the wine makes us one with Christ. In the more modern language of James Foley's hymn, we sing,

> One bread, one body, one Lord of all,
>   one cup of blessing which we bless.
> And we, though many throughout the earth,
>   we are one body in this one Lord. [10]

(c) 1978, John B. Foley, SJ and OCP Publications, 5536
NE Hassalo, Portland, OR 97213. All rights reserved.
Used with permission.

In singing these words, we express our faith and affirm our commitment to God and each other as we are joined together as the body of Christ in this sacrament. And the act does not end with the eating. In the second verse, Foley writes, "Many the gifts, many the works, / one in the Lord of all."[11] God's pilgrim people have been given many gifts to love God and neighbor, and this meal we share nourishes us to use our diverse gifts for servant ministry as we follow in Jesus' steps of love.

To break bread with others in our church is not just a personal religious experience; it signifies that *we are one with Christ and with each other in all of our diversity*. We are made one in the body of Christ as we are called to love God and our neighbor through servant ministry. This means that as the bread of Christ, we, through God's love, offer Christ's unconditional love to all of those we meet on our way. In the creative words of Frederick Buechner:

> To eat this particular meal together is to meet at the level of our most basic humanness, which involves our need not just for food but for each other. I need you to help fill my emptiness just as you need me to help fill yours. As for the emptiness that's still left over, well we're in it together, or it in us. Maybe it's what makes us human and makes us brothers [and sisters].
>
> The next time you walk down the street, take a good look at every face you pass and in your mind say *Christ died for thee*. That girl. That slob. That phony. That crook. That saint. That damned fool. *Christ* died for thee. Take and eat this in remembrance that Christ died for *thee*.[12]

Buechner's words remind us that sharing in Holy Communion binds us together in communion with Christ. This is the radical love of the great commandment—to remember that Christ died for each person we meet and to be God's love for that person.

Every time we partake in Holy Communion, God invites us anew into a deeper relationship of love. For it is *in the breaking of bread that God's love in Jesus Christ is revealed to us and experienced by us*. In the communion ritual, we are bound together as God's pilgrim people on a journey of faith. When we come to the table, we experience forgiveness for our sins and hear the call to take on the mind and mission of Christ. When we eat the bread and drink the wine, we are nourished for our ministry of serving in the world. When we leave the table, we go out as God's servant people following in Jesus' steps of love.

It is this invitation to share in this body and to go out to serve our neighbor with mercy and justice that leads others to experience the bread of Christ—God's love for them through us. Our acts of unconditional love through servant ministry not only invite others into this life of radical love for God and neighbor but also become the curriculum for forming faith. I once summed it up this way: If our aim is for persons to grow in love of God and neighbor, then a congregational ministry of making disciples must address the brokenness of injustice and oppression in the world. One of the realities of living in a world of instant communication is that we are inundated with the demands a global society places on us as individuals and as communities. How do we celebrate the diversity that surrounds us while honoring our shared commitment to Christ? If we are honest with ourselves, we might find that theological diversity is not the most difficult issue for us. Questions of religion, race, class, and sexual orientation are waiting to be addressed by those who profess faith in a God who loves all of creation. As faithful servant leaders, we must nurture disciples who seek out and combat injustice in the institutions of business, government, education, health care, and criminal justice, as well as in the church. Through Scripture and tradition, as well as through our own religious experiences, we hear God calling to us. Through the needs of our neighbors, God calls to us. The free gift of God's grace calls to us. We are called to share the vision, to see the need, to think and act. We are called to be the body of Christ, inviting others to join us in a servant communion that continues Christ's work in this world.[13]

God is calling us forward on our pilgrimage in faith to love all of creation, and God is calling us to be the bread of Christ in the world by serving others. This is the challenge: to open our lives to God's transforming grace and to respond to God's love in Jesus Christ by serving our neighbors. It is not enough to have a vision of the bread of Christ; we are *called to be the bread of Christ* for those who are abused and hurting in this world. To remember God's love given for us in Jesus Christ and made present to us by the Holy Spirit and to be that love for others is the curriculum for forming faith. In the sacrament of the bread and wine is the beginning of a congregational ministry of making disciples.

Toward Creating a Congregational Ministry of Making Disciples

THE CHALLENGES THAT LIE AHEAD

Discuss the main ideas of this chapter with your planning team for a congregational ministry of making disciples. What insights have you gained? What questions do you have?

Challenges
- We need to learn to focus on our shared commitment to Christ while we celebrate the diversity among us.
- We are not to share our God-given gifts for our own gain but for the benefit of others in love.
- Our vision and knowledge of God is only partial.

Moving Forward in Love
- Create a vision.
- Build communion.
- Organize for cultivating outer and inner lives of faith.
- Assess the need.
- Act.

The Bread of Christ
- God calls us to become the bread of Christ for others.
- In the breaking of bread, God's love in Jesus Christ is revealed to us and experienced by us.
- We are one with Christ *and* with each other in all of our diversity.

Other Suggestions for Reflecting and Planning

These suggestions can be used for individual reflection, for discussion in a Christian education event for youth or adults, or for sharing with a team who is designing a congregational ministry of making disciples.

1. Share your experiences of participating in Holy Communion during your life. What does it mean to you? How has this sacrament shaped your life of faith?

2. Share Holy Communion sitting around a table together. Talk about Christ as the bread of life and what that means to you. Share examples of where you have seen persons being the bread of life for others in situations of oppression and injustice.

3. Use the tools for planning a congregational ministry of forming faith in Appendixes I-IV. They could be completed individually or in a group and then shared with the team who is designing a congregational ministry of making disciples.

Additional Reading for This Chapter

Challenges Ahead

Fishburn, Janet F., ed. *People of a Compassionate God: Creating Welcoming Congregations*. Nashville: Abingdon Press, 2003.

Friedman, Thomas L. *The World Is Flat: A Brief History of the Twenty-First Century*. Updated and expanded edition. New York: Farrar, Strauss & Giroux, 2006.

Moore, Mary Elizabeth. *Ministering with the Earth*. St. Louis: Chalice Press, 1998.

Palmer, Parker J. *The Courage to Teach: Exploring the Inner Landscape of a Teacher's Life*. San Francisco: Jossey-Bass, 1998.

Nourishing the Spiritual Life

Edwards, Tilden. *Living in the Present: Disciplines for the Spiritual Heart*. San Francisco: Harper & Row, 1987.

———. *Living Simply Through the Day: Spiritual Survival in a Complex Age*. New York: Paulist Press, 1977.

Harris, Maria. *Dance of the Spirit: The Seven Steps of Women's Spirituality*. New York: Bantam Books, 1989.

APPENDIX I
Purpose and Goals

Write your own statement of purpose and goals for a congregational ministry of forming faith.

A P P E N D I X   I I
Assessment of Congregational Life

1. List relationships, structures, and experiences where persons could find these things in the life of your congregation.

AUTHENTIC RELATIONSHIP	FAITHFUL COMMUNITY	DEEPER MEANING

2. List relationships, structures, and experiences that build communion in these areas of your congregational life.

WORSHIP	TEACHING	CARE	FELLOWSHIP	SERVICE

3. In the column on the left, list areas of the church's life, and then describe activities and experiences that contribute to making connections, engaging the story, and sharing a vision. Note: I've provided some examples, but you need to itemize all the structures and learning activities under each on the chart that you create (for example, administration: governing council, trustees, finance, and ministerial staff). Try to see how many elements you can identify in your congregation's life and name how each contributes to this process. You could divide up the list and have the persons who serve in the nurture ministries fill out a chart for their area, for example. But it would be helpful to have some persons who do not serve in leadership in that area to fill out a chart for nurture as well. This would help you see where there are differences in perception.

	Making Connections	Engaging the Story	Sharing a Vision
Worship			
Nurture			
Outreach			
Administration			

Servant Mentors

Who Shall Teach?
Qualities

1. True dedication to God and to the nurturing of others on the pilgrimage of faith.

2. Knowledge of the Christian tradition and denominational beliefs and practice.

3. Commitment to the Christian discipline of nurturing one's own inner and outer life through the practice of faith through spiritual disciplines, studying the Christian tradition, and serving others.

4. Ability to work with a diverse group of people, recognizing the necessity of diversity for discovering God's truth for our lives of faith.

5. Life pattern of servant ministry, embodying the life of Christ by loving God and all of God's creation.

6. Evidence of continued growth in communion with God and neighbor through servant leadership.

Make a list of persons who exhibit these qualities of servant teaching and note where they are currently serving in the life of your congregation or community.

Relationships, Structures, and Practices for Forming Faith

Fill in the chart with relationships, structures, and practices that are already available in your congregational life and then add those that you would like to create.

INVITATION TO COMMUNION	DEEPENING COMMUNION	FULL COMMUNION
How to Teach?	**How to Teach?**	**How to Teach?**
Relationships: Individual counsel	**Relationships:** Individual counsel	**Relationships:** Individual counsel
Instructional mentoring Honest conversation Reflection on practice	Dialogical mentoring Honest conversation Reflection on practice	Mutual mentoring Honest conversation Reflection on practice
Cultivating the Inner Life of Faith Structures:	**Cultivating the Inner Life of Faith Structures:**	**Cultivating the Inner Life of Faith Structures:**

Practices:	**Practices:**	**Practices:**
Cultivating the Outer Life of Faith *Structures:*	**Cultivating the Outer Life of Faith** *Structures:*	**Cultivating the Outer Life of Faith** *Structures:*
Practices:	**Practices:**	**Practices:**
Christian / Christian Tradition Practice	**Christian - Christian Tradition Practice**	**Christian \ Christian Tradition Practice**

Notes

Introduction

1. Modified from Sondra Higgins Matthaei, *Making Disciples: Faith Formation in the Wesleyan Tradition* (Nashville: Abingdon Press, 2000), 170–71.

1. Relationship, Communion, and Meaning

1. Parker J. Palmer, *To Know as We Are Known: A Spirituality of Education* (San Francisco: Harper & Row, 1983), 73–74.

2. Ibid., 74.

3. Laurent A. Daloz, *Mentor: Guiding the Journey of Adult Learners* (San Francisco: Jossey-Bass, 1999), 206.

4. John D. Zizioulas, *Being as Communion* (Crestwood, N.Y.: St. Vladimir's Seminary Press, 1993), 105.

5. Erik Erikson, *Identity and the Life Cycle* (New York: W. W. Norton, 1959), 57.

6. Parker J. Palmer, *The Promise of Paradox: A Celebration of Contradictions in the Christian Life* (Notre Dame, Ind.: Ave Maria Press, 1980), 74.

7. Nelle Morton, *The Journey Is Home* (Boston: Beacon Press, 1985), 205.

8. Anne Leo Ellis, *First, We Must Listen: Living in a Multicultural Society* (New York: Friendship Press, 1996), 7.

9. Evelyn Eaton Whitehead and James D. Whitehead, *Community of Faith: Models and Strategies for Developing Christian Communities* (New York: Seabury Press, 1982), 24.

10. Ibid.

11. Ibid., 25.

12. Palmer, *The Promise of Paradox*, 82.

13. Zizioulas, *Being as Communion*, 212.

14. Charles R. Foster, *Educating Congregations: The Future of Christian Education* (Nashville: Abingdon Press, 1994), 93.

15. Jack Mezirow, *Transformative Dimensions of Adult Learning* (San Francisco: Jossey-Bass, 1991), 10.

16. Margaret Ann Crain and Jack Seymour, *Yearning for God: Reflections of Faithful Lives* (Nashville: Upper Room Books, 2003), 10.

17. Morton, *The Journey Is Home*, 41.

18. Frances Taylor Gench, *Back to the Well: Women's Encounters with Jesus in the Gospels* (Louisville: Westminster/John Knox, 2004), 112.

19. Ibid., 111.

20. Ibid., 117.

21. Ibid.

22. John Wesley, Sermon 2, "The Almost Christian" (1741), in *Sermons I: 1–33* (vol. 1 of *The Works of John Wesley*, ed. Albert C. Outler; Nashville: Abingdon Press, 1984), 137–38 (inclusive language mine). I have changed John Wesley's language because of his recognition of the shared faith of all Christians and his growing awareness of the need for more inclusive language in relation to gender. As Randy Maddox observed, John Wesley remained a "man of his time," but he did demonstrate a beginning awareness of exclusive language when he changed "Christian men" to "Christian" in an edited work. Randy Maddox, *Responsible Grace: John Wesley's Practical Theology* (Nashville: Kingswood Books, 1994), 259n22.

23. Warren Carter, "Love God, Love Neighbor: Societal Vision in Matthew 22:34–40," in Sondra Higgins Matthaei, ed., *Loving God, Loving Neighbor: Ministry with Questioning Youth* (Philadelphia: Xlibris, 2008).

2. Forming Faith in a Communion of Grace

1. John Wesley, Sermon 2, "The Almost Christian" (1741), in *Sermons I: 1–33* (vol. 1 of *The Works of John Wesley*, ed. Albert C. Outler; Nashville: Abingdon Press, 1984), 137–38.

2. John Wesley, "The Character of a Methodist" (1742) in *The Methodist Societies: History, Nature, and Design* (vol. 9 of *The Works of John Wesley*, ed. Rupert E. Davies; Nashville: Abingdon Press, 1989), 41.

3. Ibid., 33–34. Wesley would probably agree that these marks apply to most Christians, but this was a teaching document for those who were part of the early Methodist movement.

4. Ibid., 34.

5. This is a paraphrase of marks of the Christian life named by Wesley as "avoiding all harm" and doing "good unto all." Ibid., 41.

6. Thomas Groome, *Christian Religious Education: Sharing Our Story and Vision* (San Francisco: Harper & Row, 1980), 14.

7. Nelle Morton, *The Journey Is Home* (Boston: Beacon Press, 1985), xviii.

8. Groome, *Christian Religious Education*, 15.

9. John Westerhoff, *Will Our Children Have Faith?* (New York: Seabury, 1976), 193.

10. Horace Bushnell, *Christian Nurture* (Grand Rapids: Baker Book House, 1984; reprint of the 1861 edition published by Charles Scribner), 10.

11. Westerhoff, *Will Our Children Have Faith?* 193.

12. Ibid., 89.

13. James Fowler, *Stages of Faith: The Psychology of Human Development and the Quest for Meaning* (San Francisco: Harper & Row, 1981), 121.

14. Ibid., 133.

15. Ibid., 149.

16. Ibid., 173.

17. Ibid., 182.

18. Ibid., 198.

19. Ibid., 199, 201.

20. Maria Harris and Gabriel Moran, "Educating Persons," in Jack L. Seymour, ed., *Mapping Christian Education: Approaches to Congregational Learning* (Nashville: Abingdon Press, 1997), 69–70.

21. Sondra Higgins Matthaei, *Making Disciples: Faith Formation in the Wesleyan Tradition* (Nashville: Abingdon Press, 2000), 62–64.

22. Ibid., 64–65.

23. Harris and Moran, "Educating Persons," 66.

24. Ibid., 70.

25. Richard B. Hays, "First Corinthians" in *Interpretation: A Bible Commentary for Teaching and Preaching* (James Luther Mays, ed.; Louisville: Westminster John Knox Press, 1997), 215.

26. Ibid.

27. Ibid.

28. James D. G. Dunn, *The Theology of Paul the Apostle* (Grand Rapids: Eerdmans, 1998), 551.

29. Jürgen Moltmann, "Perichoresis: An Old Magic Word for a New Trinitarian Theology" in *Trinity, Community, and Power: Mapping Trajectories in Wesleyan Theology* (ed. M. Douglas Meeks; Nashville: Kingswood Books, 2000), 114, 117.

30. Ibid., 114.

31. Ibid.

32. This proposal is developed more fully in Sondra Higgins Matthaei, *Faith Matters: Faith-Mentoring in the Faith Community* (Valley Forge, Pa.: Trinity Press International, 1996).

33. Eric H. F. Law, *Inclusion: Making Room for Grace* (St. Louis: Chalice Press, 2000), xii.

34. Ibid., 43.

35. For an important study and discussion on intentionally welcoming diversity in a congregation see Charles R. Foster and Theodore Brelsford, *We Are the Church Together: Cultural Diversity in Congregational Life* (Valley Forge, Pa.: Trinity Press International, 1996).

36. Hays, "First Corinthians," 216.

37. My thanks to the Reverend Gregg Sealey for suggesting this question.

3. Following in the Steps of Love

1. Joel B. Green, *The Gospel of Luke* (Grand Rapids: Eerdmans, 1997), 766.

2. Ibid., 767.

3. Ibid.

4. Ibid., 768

5. Sondra Higgins Matthaei, *Faith Matters: Faith-Mentoring in the Faith Community* (Valley Forge, Pa.: Trinity Press International, 1996), 14.

6. Some material in this section has been revised from its previous use in Sondra Higgins Matthaei, "The United Methodist Deacon: Servant Ministry in the Communion of the Trinity" (Nashville: General Board of Higher Education and Ministry of the United Methodist Church, 2003).

7. R. Eduard Schweizer, "Ministry in the Early Church" in vol. 4 of *The Anchor Bible Dictionary* (ed. David Noel Freedman; New York: Doubleday, 1992), 835.

8. Ibid., 836 (emphasis mine).

9. Warren Carter, "Getting Martha out of the Kitchen: Luke 10:38-42 Again," in *A Feminist Companion to Luke* (ed. Amy-Jill Levine with Marianne Blickenstaff; London: Sheffield Academic Press, 2002), 223. An error in the text has been corrected by using the first publication of this chapter in *Catholic Biblical Quarterly* 58, no. 2 (April 1996): 272.

10. Sondra Higgins Matthaei, "In the Steps of Love: For Kathryn upon Her Ordination as Deacon" (sermon, The Cathedral of All Souls, Asheville, N.C., May 6, 2006).

11. Gayle Carlton Felton, *By Water and the Spirit: Making Connections for Identity and Ministry* (Nashville: Discipleship Resources, 1997), 17–18.

12. From ¶125 of *The Book of Discipline of the United Methodist Church—2004* (Nashville: The United Methodist Publishing House, 2004).

13. This helpful phrase was used by Kenneth Howcroft in distinguishing the particular roles for orders of ministry in his articulation of the theology of ministry for the British Methodist Church in "New Creation and Christian Formation: Changed from Glory into Glory as Church and Ministers," Eleventh Oxford Institute on Methodist Theological Studies, August 2002, 13.

14. *The Book of Common Prayer* (New York: Seabury Press, 1977), 543.

15. Victor Paul Furnish, *The Anchor Bible: II Corinthians* (Garden City, N.Y.: Doubleday, 1984), 197, 334.

16. Ibid., 413.

17. *Book of Discipline*, ¶¶221, 328.

18. John Wesley felt that parents, teachers, and leaders should be models of the Christian life. In instructing parents about education of girls, he recommended that parents "send them to some mistress that truly fears God, *one whose life is a pattern to her scholars*." John Wesley, Sermon 94, "On Family Religion" (1783), in *Sermons III: 71–114* (vol. 3 of *The Works of John Wesley*, ed. Albert C. Outler; Nashville: Abingdon Press, 1986), 343 (emphasis mine).

19. *Book of Discipline*, ¶328.

20. Howcroft, "New Creation and Christian Formation," 13.

21. *Book of Discipline*, ¶328.

22. Howcroft, "New Creation and Christian Formation," 11.

23. Ibid., 12.

24. Thomas Edward Frank, *Polity, Practice, and the Mission of The United Methodist Church* (Nashville: Abingdon Press, 1997), 42.

25. John N. Collins, *Diakonia: Re-interpreting the Ancient Sources* (New York: Oxford University Press, 1990), 47.

26. Green, *Gospel of Luke*, 766.

27. Robert K. Greenleaf, *Servant Leadership: A Journey into the Nature of Legitimate Power and Greatness* (New York: Paulist Press, 1977), 7.

28. Greenleaf, *Servant Leadership*, 13.

29. www.wordreference.com/definition/leader. Accessed May 23, 2007.

30. Matthaei, *Faith Matters*, 66.

31. Ibid., 52.

32. Greenleaf, *Servant Leadership*, 15.

33. Ibid., 17.

34. Ibid., 21.

35. "We Are the Church," *The United Methodist Hymnal* (Nashville: The United Methodist Publishing House, 1989), 558 (emphasis mine).

36. One resource that is particularly helpful in terms of a process for engaging the story is a book by Anne Streaty Wimberly, *Soul Stories: African American Christian Education* (rev. ed.; Nashville: Abingdon Press, 2005). The method of reflection grows out of the African American church but can be modified for any group wanting to reflect more deeply on experiences of faith.

37. See Eric H. F. Law's respectful communication guidelines at the end of this chapter. From *The Bush Was Blazing But Not Consumed: Developing Multicultural Community through Dialogue Liturgy* (St. Louis: Chalice Press, 1996), 87.

38. For proposals about how to create the intersection between God's Story and an individual story, see Thomas Groome, *Christian Religious Education: Sharing Our Story and Vision* (San Francisco: Harper & Row, 1980) and Wimberly, *Soul Stories*.

39. Law, *Bush Was Blazing*, 87.

40. Eric H. F. Law, *The Wolf Shall Dwell with the Lamb: A Spirituality for Leadership in a Multicultural Community* (St. Louis: Chalice Press, 1993), 82–83.

4. Growing in Communion with God and All of Creation

1. Gordon D. Fee, *The New International Commentary on the New Testament: The First Epistle to the Corinthians* (Grand Rapids: Eerdmans, 1987), 48, 122.

2. Ibid., 122.

3. Roberta Bondi, *To Love as God Loves* (Minneapolis: Augsburg Fortress, 1987), 101.

4. Maria Harris, *Fashion Me a People: Curriculum in the Church* (Louisville: Westminster/John Knox, 1989), 8, 24–25.

5. John Westerhoff was an early proponent of this approach in *Living the Faith Community: The Church that Makes a Difference* (Minneapolis: Winston Press, 1985).

6. For a full discussion of the question *Who shall teach?* in the early Methodist movement, see Sondra Higgins Matthaei, *Making Disciples: Faith Formation in the Wesleyan Tradition* (Nashville: Abingdon Press, 2000), 99–122.

7. James D. G. Dunn, *The Theology of Paul the Apostle* (Grand Rapids: Eerdmans, 1998), 552.

8. Ibid., 553.

9. Ibid., 554.

10. Ibid.

11. Ibid., 559.

12. Fee, *The First Epistle to the Corinthians*, 627.

13. Dunn, *Theology of Paul the Apostle*, 560.

14. Matthaei, *Making Disciples*, 25.

15. Robert A. Evans, "Education for Emancipation: Movement Toward Transformation," in Alice Frazer Evans, Robert A. Evans, and William Bean Kennedy, *Pedagogies for the Non-Poor* (Maryknoll, N.Y.: Orbis Books, 1987), 259.

16. These roles were first discussed in Sondra Higgins Matthaei, "An Ecology of Formation in the Wesleyan Tradition," 1998 *Proceedings* of the Annual Meeting of the Association of Professors and Researchers in Religious Education and the Religious Education Association Biennial Conference, 107. The discussion is more fully developed in Matthaei, *Making Disciples*, 26–28.

17. James Fowler, *Becoming Adult, Becoming Christian* (San Francisco: Harper & Row, 1984), 95.

18. Frederick Buechner, *Wishful Thinking: A Seeker's ABC* (San Francisco: Harper & Row, 1993), 119.

19. The following figures have been modified from those in Matthaei, *Making Disciples*, 69, 95, 121, 142, and 160.

20. Charles R. Foster. *Educating Congregations: The Future of Christian Education* (Nashville: Abingdon Press, 1994).

5. The Challenges That Lie Ahead

1. Gordon D. Fee, *The New International Commentary on the New Testament: The First Epistle to the Corinthians* (Grand Rapids: Eerdmans, 1987), 641.

2. Ibid., 642.

3. Ibid., 646.

4. Ibid., 648.

5. Maria Rainer Rilke, *Letters to a Young Poet* (trans. M. D. Herter Norton; New York: W. W. Norton, 1993), 35.

6. Fee, *The First Epistle to the Corinthians*, 650.

7. Ibid., 651.

8. Sondra Higgins Matthaei, *Making Disciples: Faith Formation in the Wesleyan Tradition* (Nashville: Abingdon Press, 2000), 182.

9. James D. G. Dunn, *The Theology of Paul the Apostle* (Grand Rapids: Eerdmans, 1998), 550.

10. "One Bread, One Body," *The United Methodist Hymnal* (Nashville: The United Methodist Publishing House, 1989), 620.

11. Ibid.

12. Frederick Buechner, "Lord's Supper," *Alive Now* (Sept./Oct. 1976): 57.

13. Adapted from Matthaei, *Making Disciples*, 182–83.

Works Cited

Bellah, Robert N., Richard Madsen, William M. Sullivan, Ann Swidler, and Stephen M. Tipton, *Habits of the Heart: Individualism and Commitment in American Life*. Berkeley: University of California Press, 1985.

Bondi, Roberta. *To Love as God Loves*. Minneapolis: Augsburg Fortress, 1987.

The Book of Common Prayer. New York: Seabury Press, 1977.

Book of Discipline of the United Methodist Church—2004. Nashville: The United Methodist Publishing House, 2004.

Buechner, Frederick. "Lord's Supper." *Alive Now* (Sept./Oct. 1976).

———. *Wishful Thinking: A Seeker's ABC*. San Francisco: Harper & Row, 1993.

Bushnell, Horace. *Christian Nurture*. New York: Charles Scribner, 1861. Reprint, Grand Rapids: Baker Book House, 1984.

Carter, Warren. "Getting Martha Out of the Kitchen: Luke 10:38-42 Again." Pages 215–31 in *A Feminist Companion to Luke*. Edited by Amy-Jill Levine with Marianne Blickenstaff. London: Sheffield Academic Press, 2002.

———. "Getting Martha out of the Kitchen: Luke 10:38-42 Again." *Catholic Biblical Quarterly* 58, no. 2 (April 1996): 264–80.

———. "Love God, Love Neighbor: Societal Vision in Matthew 22:34-40." In *Loving God, Loving Neighbor: Ministry with Questioning Youth*. Edited by Sondra Higgins Matthaei. Philadelphia: Xlibris, 2008.

Collins, John N. *Diakonia: Re-interpreting the Ancient Sources*. New York: Oxford University Press, 1990.

Crain, Margaret Ann, and Jack Seymour. *Yearning for God: Reflections of Faithful Lives*. Nashville: Upper Room Books, 2003.

Daloz, Laurent A. *Mentor: Guiding the Journey of Adult Learners*. San Francisco: Jossey-Bass, 1999.

Dunn, James D. G. *The Theology of Paul the Apostle*. Grand Rapids: Eerdmans, 1998.

Ellis, Anne Leo. *First, We Must Listen: Living in a Multicultural Society*. New York: Friendship Press, 1996.

English, Leona M. *Mentoring in Religious Education*. Birmingham: Religious Education Press, 1998.

Erikson, Erik. *Identity and the Life Cycle*. New York: W. W. Norton, 1959.

Evans, Robert A. "Education for Emancipation: Movement Toward Transformation." Pages 257–84 in Alice Frazer Evans, Robert A. Evans, and William Bean Kennedy, *Pedagogies for the Non-Poor*. Maryknoll, N.Y.: Orbis Books, 1987.

Fee, Gordon D. *The New International Commentary on the New Testament: The First Epistle to the Corinthians*. Grand Rapids: Eerdmans, 1987.

Felton, Gayle Carlton. *By Water and the Spirit: Making Connections for Identity and Ministry*. Nashville: Discipleship Resources, 1997.

Foley, James B., "One Bread, One Body" (1978). In *The United Methodist Hymnal*. Nashville: United Methodist Publishing House, 1989, 620.

Foster, Charles R. *Educating Congregations: The Future of Christian Education*. Nashville: Abingdon Press, 1994.

Foster, Charles R., and Theodore Brelsford. *We Are the Church Together: Cultural Diversity in Congregational Life*. Valley Forge, Pa.: Trinity Press International, 1996.

Fowler, James. *Becoming Adult, Becoming Christian*. San Francisco: Harper & Row, 1984.

———. *Stages of Faith: The Psychology of Human Development and the Quest for Meaning*. San Francisco: Harper & Row, 1981.

Frank, Thomas Edward. *Polity, Practice, and the Mission of The United Methodist Church*. Nashville: Abingdon Press, 1997.

Furnish, Victor Paul. *The Anchor Bible: II Corinthians*. Garden City, N.Y.: Doubleday, 1984.

Gench, Frances Taylor, *Back to the Well: Women's Encounters with Jesus in the Gospels*. Louisville: Westminster/John Knox, 2004.

Green, Joel B. *The Gospel of Luke*. Grand Rapids: Eerdmans, 1997.

Greenleaf, Robert K. *Servant Leadership: A Journey into the Nature of Legitimate Power and Greatness*. New York: Paulist Press, 1977.

Groome, Thomas. *Christian Religious Education: Sharing Our Story and Vision*. San Francisco: Harper & Row, 1980.

Harris, Maria. *Fashion Me a People: Curriculum in the Church*. Louisville: Westminster/John Knox, 1989.

Harris, Maria, and Gabriel Moran, "Educating Persons." Pages 58–73 in *Mapping Christian Education: Approaches to Congregational Learning*. Edited by Jack L. Seymour. Nashville: Abingdon Press, 1997.

Hays, Richard B. "First Corinthians." In *Interpretation: A Bible Commentary for Teaching and Preaching*. Edited by James Luther Mays. Louisville: Westminster John Knox Press, 1997.

Howcroft, Kenneth. "New Creation and Christian Formation: Changed from Glory into Glory as Church and Ministers." Paper presented at the Eleventh Oxford Institute on Methodist Theological Studies, August, 2002.

Law, Eric H. F. *The Bush Was Blazing But Not Consumed: Developing Multicultural Community through Dialogue Liturgy*. St. Louis: Chalice Press, 1996.

———. *Inclusion: Making Room for Grace*. St. Louis: Chalice Press, 2000.

————. *The Wolf Shall Dwell with the Lamb: A Spirituality for Leadership in a Multicultural Community.* St. Louis: Chalice Press, 1993.

Maddox, Randy. *Responsible Grace: John Wesley's Practical Theology.* Nashville: Kingswood Books, 1994.

Matthaei, Sondra Higgins. "An Ecology of Formation in the Wesleyan Tradition." *Proceedings* of the Annual Meeting of the Association of Professors and Researchers in Religious Education and the Religious Education Association Biennial Conference, 1998.

————. "In the Steps of Love: For Kathryn upon Her Ordination as Deacon." Sermon, The Cathedral of All Souls, Asheville, N.C., May 6, 2006.

————. "The United Methodist Deacon: Servant Ministry in the Communion of the Trinity." Nashville: General Board of Higher Education and Ministry of the United Methodist Church, 2003.

————. *Faith Matters: Faith-Mentoring in the Faith Community.* Valley Forge, Pa.: Trinity Press International, 1996.

————. *Making Disciples: Faith Formation in the Wesleyan Tradition.* Nashville: Abingdon Press, 2000.

Mezirow, Jack. *Transformative Dimensions of Adult Learning.* San Francisco: Jossey-Bass, 1991.

Moltmann, Jürgen. "Perichoresis: An Old Magic Word for a New Trinitarian Theology." Pages 111–26 in *Trinity, Community, and Power: Mapping Trajectories in Wesleyan Theology.* Edited by M. Douglas Meeks. Nashville: Kingswood Books, 2000.

Moore, Mary Elizabeth Mullino. *Teaching as a Sacramental Act.* Cleveland: Pilgrim Press, 2004.

Morton, Nelle. *The Journey Is Home.* Boston: Beacon Press, 1985.

Palmer, Parker J. *The Courage to Teach: Exploring the Inner Landscape of a Teacher's Life.* San Francisco: Jossey-Bass, 1998.

————. *The Promise of Paradox: A Celebration of Contradictions in the Christian Life.* Notre Dame, Ind.: Ave Maria Press, 1980.

————. *To Know as We Are Known: A Spirituality of Education.* San Francisco: Harper & Row, 1983.

Rilke, Maria Rainer, *Letters to a Young Poet.* Translated by M. D. Herter Norton. New York: W. W. Norton, 1993.

Schweizer, R. Eduard. "Ministry in the Early Church." Pages 835–42 in vol. 4 of *The Anchor Bible Dictionary.* Edited by David Noel Freedman. New York: Doubleday, 1992.

Wesley, John. "The Character of a Methodist." Pages 31–46 in *The Methodist Societies: History, Nature, and Design.* Vol. 9 of *The Works of John Wesley.* Edited by Rupert E. Davies. Nashville: Abingdon Press, 1989.

————. Sermon 2, "The Almost Christian." Pages 131–41 in *Sermons I: 1-33.* Vol. 1 of *The Works of John Wesley.* Edited by Albert C. Outler. Nashville: Abingdon Press, 1984.

————. Sermon 94, "On Family Religion." Pages 333–46 in *Sermons III: 71-114*. Vol. 3 of *The Works of John Wesley*. Edited by Albert C. Outler. Nashville: Abingdon Press, 1986.

Westerhoff, John. *Living the Faith Community: The Church that Makes a Difference*. Minneapolis: Winston Press, 1985.

————. *Will Our Children Have Faith?* New York: Seabury, 1976.

Whitehead, Evelyn Eaton, and James D. Whitehead. *Community of Faith: Models and Strategies for Developing Christian Communities*. New York: Seabury Press, 1982.

Wimberly, Anne Streaty. *Soul Stories: African American Religious Education*. Revised Edition. Nashville: Abingdon Press, 2005.

Zachary, Lois J. *The Mentor's Guide: Facilitating Effective Learning Relationships*. San Francisco: Jossey-Bass, 2000.

Zizioulas, John D. *Being as Communion*. Crestwood, N.Y.: St. Vladimir's Seminary Press, 1993.

Index